THE WORKS OF JAMES WHITCOMB RILEY ❧ ❧
VOL. X

THE POEMS AND PROSE
❧ ❧ SKETCHES OF ❧ ❧
JAMES WHITCOMB RILEY

A CHILD-WORLD

CHARLES SCRIBNER'S
SONS ❧ NEW YORK ❧ 1904

TO

MR. AND MRS. CHARLES L. HOLSTEIN

CONTENTS

CONTENTS

A CHILD-WORLD

The Child-World—long and long since lost to view—
A Fairy Paradise!—
How always fair it was and fresh and new—
How every affluent hour heaped heart and eyes
With treasures of surprise!

Enchantments tangible: The under-brink
Of dawns that launched the sight
Up seas of gold: The dewdrop on the pink,
With all the green earth in it and blue height
Of heavens infinite:

The liquid, dripping songs of orchard-birds—
The wee bass of the bees,—
With lucent deeps of silence afterwards;
The gay, clandestine whisperings of the breeze
And glad leaves of the trees.

.   .   .   .

O Child-World: After this world—just as when
I found you first sufficed
My soulmost need—if I found you again,
With all my childish dream so realized,
I should not be surprised.

THE CHILD-WORLD

A CHILD-WORLD, yet a wondrous world no less,
To those who knew its boundless happiness.
A simple old frame house—eight rooms in all—
Set just one side the centre of a small
But very hopeful Indiana town,—
The upper story looking squarely down
Upon the main street, and the main highway
From East to West,—historic in its day,
Known as The National Road—old-timers, all
Who linger yet, will happily recall
It as the scheme and handiwork, as wel
As property, of "Uncle Sam," and tell
Of its importance, "long and long afore
*Rail*roads wuz ever *dreamp'* of!"—Furthermore.
The reminiscent first inhabitants
Will make that old road blossom with romance
Of snowy caravans, in long parade
Of covered vehicles, of every grade

3

From ox-cart of most primitive design,
To Conestoga wagons, with their fine
Deep-chested six-horse teams, in heavy gear,
High hames and chiming bells—to childish ear
And eye entrancing as the glittering train
Of some sun-smitten pageant of old Spain.
And, in like spirit, haply they will tell
You of the roadside forests, and the yell
Of "wolfs" and "painters," in the long night-
    ride,
And "screechin' catamounts" on every side.—
Of stage-coach days, highwaymen, and strange
    crimes,
And yet unriddled mysteries of the times
Called "Good Old." "And why 'Good Old'?" once
    a rare
Old chronicler was asked, who brushed the hair
Out of his twinkling eyes and said,—"Well, John,
They're 'good old times' because they're dead and
    gone!"

The old home site was portioned into three
Distinctive lots. The front one—natively
Facing to southward, broad and gaudy-fine
With lilac, dahlia, rose, and flowering vine—

The dwelling stood in; and behind that, and
Upon the alley north and south, left hand,
The old woodhouse,—half, trimly stacked with
    wood,
And half, a workshop, where a work-bench stood
Steadfastly through all seasons.—Over it,
Along the wall, hung compass, brace-and-bit,
And square, and drawing-knife, and smoothing-
    plane—
And little jack-plane, too—the children's vain
Possession by pretence—in fancy they
Manipulating it in endless play,
Turning out countless curls and loops of bright,
Fine satin shavings—Rapture infinite!
Shelved quilting-frames; the tool-chest; the old box
Of refuse nails and screws; a rough gun-stock's
Outline in "curly maple"; and a pair
Of clamps and old kraut-cutter hanging there.
Some "patterns," in thin wood, of shield and scroll,
Hung higher, with a neat "cane fishing-pole"
And careful tackle—all securely out
Of reach of children, rummaging about.

Beside the woodhouse, with broad branches free
Yet close above the roof, an apple-tree

5

Known as "The Prince's Harvest"—Magic phrase!
That was *a boy's own tree*, in many ways!—
Its girth and height meet both for the caress
Of his bare legs and his ambitiousness:
And then its apples, humoring his whim,
Seemed just to fairly *hurry* ripe for him—
Even in June, impetuous as he,
They dropped to meet him, half-way up the tree.
And O their bruised sweet faces where they fell!—
And ho! the lips that feigned to "kiss them *well*"!

"The Old Sweet-Apple-Tree," a stalwart, stood
In fairly sympathetic neighborhood
Of this wild princeling with his early gold
To toss about so lavishly nor hold
In bounteous hoard to overbrim at once
All Nature's lap when came the Autumn months.
Under the spacious shade of this the eyes
Of swinging children saw swift-changing skies
Of blue and green, with sunshine shot between,
And when "the old cat died" they saw but green.

And, then, there was a cherry-tree.—We all
And severally will yet recall

From our lost youth, in gentlest memory,
The blessed fact—There was a cherry-tree.

There was a cherry-tree.   Its bloomy snows
Cool even now the fevered sight that knows
No more its airy visions of pure joy—
    As when you were a boy.

There was a cherry-tree.   The Blue Jay set
His blue against its white—O blue as jet
He seemed there then!—But *now*—Whoever knew
    He was so pale a blue!

There was a cherry-tree—Our child-eyes saw
The miracle:—Its pure-white snows did thaw
Into a crimson fruitage, far too sweet
    But for a boy to eat.

There was a cherry-tree, give thanks and joy!—
There was a bloom of snow—There was a boy—
There was a Blue Jay of the realest blue—
    And fruit for both of you.

Then the old garden, with the apple-trees
Grouped round the margin, and "a stand of bees"
By the "white-winter-pearmain"; and a row
Of currant-bushes; and a quince or so.

The old grape-arbor in the centre, by
The pathway to the stable, with the sty
Behind it, and *upon* it, cootering flocks
Of pigeons,—and the cutest "martin-box"!—
Made like a sure-enough house—with roof, and
    doors
And windows in it, and veranda-floors
And balusters all round it—yes, and at
Each end a chimney—painted red at that
And pencilled white, to look like little bricks;
And, to cap all the builder's cunning tricks,
Two tiny little lightning-rods were run
Straight up their sides, and twinkled in the sun.
Who built it? Nay, no answer but a smile.—
It *may* be you can guess who, afterwhile.

Home in his stall, "Old Sorrel" munched his hay
And oats and corn, and switched the flies away,
In a repose of patience good to see,
And earnest of the gentlest pedigree.
With half-pathetic eye sometimes he gazed
Upon the gambols of a colt that grazed
Around the edges of the lot outside,
And kicked at nothing suddenly, and tried

To act grown-up and graceful and high-bred,
But dropped, *k'whop!* and scraped the buggy-shed,
Leaving a tuft of woolly, foxy hair
Under the sharp-end of a gate-hinge there.
Then, all ignobly scrambling to his feet
And whinnying a whinny like a bleat,
He would pursue himself around the lot
And—do the whole thing over, like as not! . . .
Ah! what a life of constant fear and dread
And flop and squawk and flight the chickens led!

Above the fences, either side, were seen
The neighbor-houses, set in plots of green
Door-yards and greener gardens, tree and wall
Alike whitewashed, an order in it all:
The scythe hooked in the tree-fork; and the spade
And hoe and rake and shovel all, when laid
Aside, were in their places, ready for
The hand of either the possessor or
Of any neighbor, welcome to the loan
Of any tool he might not chance to own.

THE OLD HOME-FOLKS

SUCH was the Child-World of the long ago—
The little world these children used to know:—
Johnty, the oldest, and the best, perhaps,
Of the five happy little Hoosier chaps
Inhabiting this wee world all their own.—
Johnty, the leader, with his native tone
Of grave command—a general on parade
Whose each punctilious order was obeyed
By his proud followers.

            But Johnty yet—
After all serious duties—could forget
The gravity of life to the extent,
At times, of kindling much astonishment
About him: With a quick, observant eye,
And mind and memory, he could supply
The tamest incident with liveliest mirth;
And at the most unlooked-for times on earth

Was wont to break into some travesty
On those around him—feats of mimicry
Of this one's trick of gesture—that one's walk—
Or this one's laugh—or that one's funny talk,—
The way "the watermelon-man" would try
His humor on town-folks that wouldn't buy;—
How he drove into town at morning—then
At dusk (alas!) how he drove out again.

Though these divertisements of Johnty's were
Hailed with a hearty glee and relish, there
Appeared a sense, on his part, of regret—
A spirit of remorse that would not let
Him rest for days thereafter.—Such times he,
As some boy said, "jist got too overly
Blame' good fer common boys like us, you know,
To 'sociate with—'less'n we 'ud go
And jine his church!"

              Next after Johnty came
His little towhead brother, Bud by name.—
And O how white his hair was—and how thick
His face with freckles,—and his ears, how quick
And curious and intrusive!—And how pale
The blue of his big eyes;—and how a tale

Of Giants, Trolls or Fairies, bulged them still
Bigger and bigger!—And when "Jack" would kill
The old "Four-headed Giant," Bud's big eyes
Were swollen truly into giant-size.
And Bud was apt in make-believes—would hear
His Grandma talk or read, with such an ear
And memory of both subject and big words,
That he would take the book up afterwards
And feign to "read aloud," with such success
As caused his truthful elders real distress.
But he *must* have *big words*—they seemed to
     give
Extremer range to the superlative—
That was his passion.   " My Gran'ma," he said,
One evening, after listening as she read
Some heavy old historical review—
With copious explanations thereunto
Drawn out by his inquiring turn of mind,—
"My Gran'ma she's read *all* books—ever' kind
They is, 'at tells all 'bout the land an' sea
An' Nations of the Earth!—An' she is the
Historicul-est woman ever wuz!"
(Forgive the verse's chuckling as it does
In its erratic current.—Oftentimes
The little willowy water-brook of rhymes

12

Must falter in its music, listening to
The children laughing as they used to do.)

> Who shall sing a simple ditty all about the Willow,
>> Dainty-fine and delicate as any bending spray
> That dandles high the happy bird that flutters there
>> to trill a
>> Tremulously tender song of greeting to the May.

> Ah, my lovely Willow!—Let the Waters lilt your
>> graces,—
>> They alone with limpid kisses lave your leaves
>> above,
> Flashing back your sylvan beauty, and in shady places
>> Peering up with glimmering pebbles, like the eyes
>> of love.

Next, Maymie, with her hazy cloud of hair,
And the blue skies of eyes beneath it there.
Her dignified and "little lady" airs
Of never either romping up the stairs
Or falling down them; thoughtful everyway
Of others first—The kind of child at play
That "gave up," for the rest, the ripest pear
Or peach or apple in the garden there
Beneath the trees where swooped the airy swing—
She pushing it, too glad for anything!

13

Or, in the character of hostess, she
Would entertain her friends delightfully
In her playhouse,—with strips of carpet laid
Along the garden-fence within the shade
Of the old apple-trees—where from next yard
Came the two dearest friends in her regard,
The little Crawford girls, Ella and Lu—
As shy and lovely as the lilies grew
In their idyllic home,—yet sometimes they
Admitted Bud and Alex to their play,
Who did their heavier work and helped them fix
To have a "Festibul"—and brought the bricks
And built the "stove," with a real fire and all,
And stovepipe-joint for chimney, looming tall
And wonderfully smoky—even to
Their childish aspirations, as it blew
And swooped and swirled about them till their sight
Was feverish even as their high delight.

Then Alex, with his freckles, and his freaks
Of temper, and the peach-bloom of his cheeks,
And "*amber-colored* hair"—his mother said
'Twas that, when others laughed and called it "*red*"
And Alex threw things at them—till they'd call
A truce, agreeing "'t'uzn't red *ut-tall!*"

14

But Alex was affectionate beyond
The average child, and was extremely fond
Of the paternal relatives of his,
Of whom he once made estimate like this:—
" *I'm* only got *two* brothers,—but my *Pa*
He's got most brothers'n you ever saw!—
He's got *seben* brothers!—Yes, an' they're all my
Seben Uncles!—Uncle John, an' Jim,—an' I
Got Uncle George, an' Uncle Andy, too,
An' Uncle Frank, an' Uncle Joe.—An' you
Know Uncle *Mart*.—An', all but *him*, they're great
Big mens!—An' nen's Aunt Sarah—she makes
        eight!—
I'm got *eight* uncles!—'cept Aunt Sarah *can't*
Be ist my *uncle* 'cause she's ist my *a'nt!*"

Then, next to Alex—and the last indeed
Of these five little ones of whom you read—
Was baby Lizzie, with her velvet lisp,—
As though her elfin lips had caught some wisp
Of floss between them as they strove with speech,
Which ever seemed just in, yet out of, reach—
Though what her lips missed, her dark eyes could
        say
With looks that made her meaning clear as day.

And, knowing now the children, you must know
The father and the mother they loved so:—
The father was a swarthy man, black-eyed,
Black-haired, and high of forehead; and, beside
The slender little mother, seemed in truth
A very king of men—since, from his youth,
To his hale manhood *now*—(worthy as then,—
A lawyer and a leading citizen
Of the proud little town and county-seat—
His hopes his neighbors', and their fealty sweet)—
He had known outdoor labor—rain and shine—
Bleak Winter, and bland Summer—foul and fine.
So Nature had ennobled him and set
Her symbol on him like a coronet:
His lifted brow, and frank, reliant face—
Superior of stature as of grace,—
Even the children by the spell were wrought
Up to heroics of their simple thought,
And saw him, trim of build, and lithe and
    straight
And tall, almost, as at the pasture-gate
The towering ironweed the scythe had spared
For their sakes, when The Hired Man declared
It would grow on till it became a *tree*,
With cocoanuts and monkeys in—maybe!

Yet, though the children, in their pride and awe
And admiration of the father, saw
A being so exalted—even more
Like adoration was the love they bore
The gentle mother.—Her mild, plaintive face
Was purely fair, and haloed with a grace
And sweetness luminous when joy made glad
Her features with a smile; or saintly sad
As twilight, fell the sympathetic gloom
Of any childish grief, or as a room
Were darkened suddenly, the curtain drawn
Across the window and the sunshine gone.
Her brow, below her fair hair's glimmering strands,
Seemed meetest resting-place for blessing hands
Or holiest touches of soft finger-tips
And little rose-leaf cheeks and dewy lips.

Though heavy household tasks were pitiless,
No little waist or coat or checkered dress
But knew her needle's deftness; and no skill
Matched hers in shaping plait or flounce or frill;
Or fashioning, in complicate design,
All rich embroideries of leaf and vine,
With tiniest twining tendril,—bud and bloom
And fruit, so like, one's fancy caught perfume

17

And dainty touch and taste of them, to see
Their semblance wrought in such rare verity.

Shrined in her sanctity of home and love,
And love's fond service and reward thereof,
Restore her thus, O blessed Memory!—
Throned in her rocking-chair, and on her knee
Her sewing—her work-basket on the floor
Beside her,—Springtime through the open door
Balmily stealing in and all about
The room; the bees' dim hum, and the far shout
And laughter of the children at their play,
And neighbor-children from across the way
Calling in gleeful challenge—save alone
One boy whose voice sends back no answering tone—
The boy, prone on the floor, above a book
Of pictures, with a rapt, ecstatic look—
Even as the mother's, by the selfsame spell,
Is lifted, with a light ineffable—
As though her senses caught no mortal cry,
But heard, instead, some poem going by.

The Child-heart is so strange a little thing—
    So mild—so timorously shy and small,—
When *grown-up* hearts throb, it goes scampering
    Behind the wall, nor dares peer out at all!—

18

THE OLD HOME-FOLKS

It is the veriest mouse
That hides in any house—
So wild a little thing is any Child-heart!

Child-heart!—mild heart!—
Ho, my little wild heart!—
Come up here to me out o' the dark,
Or let me come to you!

So lorn at times the Child-heart needs must be,
With never one maturer heart for friend
And comrade, whose tear-ripened sympathy
And love might lend it comfort to the end,—
Whose yearnings, aches and stings,
Over poor little things
Were pitiful as ever any Child-heart.

Child-heart!—mild heart!—
Ho, my little wild heart!—
Come up here to me out o' the dark,
Or let me come to you!

Times, too, the little Child-heart must be glad—
Being so young, nor knowing, as *we* know,
The fact from fantasy, the good from bad,
The joy from woe, the—*all* that hurts us so!
What wonder then that thus
It hides away from us?—
So weak a little thing is any Child-heart!

19

Child-heart!—mild heart!—
Ho, my little wild heart!—
Come up here to me out o' the dark,
Or let me come to you!

Nay, little Child-heart, you have never need
To fear *us;*—we are weaker far than you—
'Tis *we* who should be fearful—we indeed
Should hide us, too, as darkly as you do,—
Safe, as yourself, withdrawn,
Hearing the World roar on
Too wilful, woful, awful for the Child-heart!

Child-heart!—mild heart!—
Ho, my little wild heart!—
Come up here to me out o' the dark,
Or let me come to you!

The clock chats on confidingly; a rose
Taps at the window, as the sunlight throws
A brilliant, jostling checkerwork of shine
And shadow, like a Persian-loom design,
Across the home-made carpet—fades,—and then
The dear old colors are themselves again.
Sounds drop in visiting from everywhere—
The bluebird's and the robin's trill are there,

Their sweet liquidity diluted some
By dewy orchard-spaces they have come:
Sounds of the town, too, and the great highway—
The Mover-wagons' rumble, and the neigh
Of over-travelled horses, and the bleat
Of sheep and low of cattle through the street—
A Nation's thoroughfare of hopes and fears,
First blazed by the heroic pioneers
Who gave up old-home idols and set face
Toward the unbroken West, to found a race
And tame a wilderness now mightier than
All peoples and all tracts American.

Blent with all outer sounds, the sounds within:—
In mild remoteness falls the household din
Of porch and kitchen: the dull jar and thump
Of churning; and the " glung-glung " of the pump,
With sudden pad and skurry of bare feet
Of little outlaws, in from field or street:
The clang of kettle,—rasp of damper-ring
And bang of cook-stove door—and everything
That jingles in a busy kitchen lifts
Its individual wrangling voice and drifts
In sweetest tinny, coppery, pewtery tone
Of music hungry ear has ever known

In wildest famished yearning and conceit
Of youth, to just cut loose and eat and eat!—
The zest of hunger still incited on
To childish desperation by long-drawn
Breaths of hot, steaming, wholesome things that
    stew
And blubber, and uptilt the pot-lids, too,
Filling the sense with zestful rumors of
The dear old-fashioned dinners children love:
Redolent savorings of home-cured meats,
Potatoes, beans and cabbage; turnips, beets
And parsnips—rarest composite entire
That ever pushed a mortal child's desire
To madness by new-grated fresh, keen, sharp
Horse-radish—tang that sets the lips awarp
And watery, anticipating all
The cloyed sweets of the glorious festival.—
Still add the cinnamony, spicy scents
Of clove, nutmeg, and myriad condiments
In like-alluring whiffs that prophesy
Of sweltering pudding, cake, and custard-pie—
The swooning-sweet aroma haunting all
The house—up-stairs and down—porch, parlor, hall
And sitting-room—invading even where
The Hired Man sniffs it in the orchard-air,

22

And pauses in his pruning of the trees
To note the sun minutely and to—sneeze.

Then Cousin Rufus comes—the children hear
His hale voice in the old hall, ringing clear
As any bell.   Always he came with song
Upon his lips and all the happy throng,
Of echoes following him, even as the crowd
Of his admiring little kinsmen—proud
To have a cousin *grown*—and yet as young
Of soul and cheery as the songs he sung.

He was a student of the law—intent
Soundly to win success, with all it meant;
And so he studied—even as he played,—
With all his heart: And so it was he made
His gallant fight for fortune—through all stress
Of battle bearing him with cheeriness
And wholesome valor.

                    And the children had
Another relative who kept them glad
And joyous by his very merry ways—
As blithe and sunny as the summer days,—
Their father's youngest brother—Uncle Mart.
The old "Arabian Nights" he knew by heart—

23

"Baron Munchausen," too; and likewise "The
Swiss Family Robinson."—And when these three
Gave out, as he rehearsed them, he could go
Straight on in the same line—a steady flow
Of arabesque invention that his good
Old mother never clearly understood.
He *was* to be a *printer*—wanted, though,
To be an *actor*.—But the world was "show"
Enough for *him*,—theatric, airy, gay,—
Each day to him was jolly as a play.
And some poetic symptoms, too, in sooth,
Were certain.—And, from his apprentice youth,
He joyed in verse-quotations—which he took
Out of the old "Type Foundry Specimen Book."
He craved and courted most the favor of
The children.—They were foremost in his love;
And pleasing *them*, he pleased his own boy-
    heart
And kept it young and fresh in every part.
So was it he devised for them and wrought
To life his quaintest, most romantic thought:—
Like some lone castaway in alien seas,
He built a house up in the apple-trees,
Out in the corner of the garden, where
No man-devouring native, prowling there,

Might pounce upon them in the dead o' night—
For lo, their little ladder, slim and light,
They drew up after them.   And it was known
That Uncle Mart slipped up sometimes alone
And drew the ladder in, to lie and moon
Over some novel all the afternoon.
And one time Johnty, from the crowd below,—
Outraged to find themselves deserted so—
Threw bodily their old black cat up in
The airy fastness, with much yowl and din
Resulting, while a wild periphery
Of cat went circling to another tree,
And, in impassioned outburst, Uncle Mart
Loomed up, and thus relieved his tragic
      heart:

" ' *Hence, long-tailed, ebon-eyed, nocturnal ranger!*
  What led thee hither 'mongst the types and cases?
  Didst thou not know that running midnight races
O'er standing types was fraught with imminent
    danger?
Did hunger lead thee—didst thou think to find
  Some rich old cheese to fill thy hungry maw?
  Vain hope! for none but literary jaw
Can masticate our cookery for the mind! ' "

So likewise when, with lordly air and grace,
He strode to dinner, with a tragic face
With ink-spots on it from the office, he .
Would aptly quote more "Specimen-poetry—"
Perchance like "'Labor's bread is sweet to eat,
(*Ahem!*) And toothsome is the toiler's meat.'"

Ah, could you see them *all*, at lull of noon!—
A sort of *boisterous* lull, with clink of spoon
And clatter of deflecting knife, and plate
Dropped saggingly, with its all-bounteous weight,
And dragged in place voraciously; and then
Pent exclamations, and the lull again.—
The garland of glad faces round the board—
Each member of the family restored
To his or her place, with an extra chair
Or two for the chance guests so often there.—
The father's farmer-client, brought home from
The court-room, though he "didn't *want* to come
Tel he jist saw he *hat* to!" he'd explain,
Invariably, time and time again,
To the pleased wife and hostess, as she pressed
Another cup of coffee on the guest.—
Or there was Johnty's special chum, perchance,
Or Bud's, or both—each childish countenance

Lit with a higher glow of youthful glee,
To be together thus unbrokenly,—
Jim Offutt, or Eck Skinner, or George Carr—
The very nearest chums of Bud's these are,—
So, very probably, *one* of the three,
At least, is there with Bud, or *ought* to be.
Like interchange the town-boys each had
     known—
His playmate's dinner better than his own—
Yet blest that he was ever made to stay
At *Almon Keefer's, any* blessed day,
For *any* meal! . . . Visions of biscuits, hot
And flaky-perfect, with the golden blot
Of molten butter for the centre, clear,
Through pools of clover-honey—*dear-o-dear!*—
With creamy milk for its divine "farewell":
And then, if any one delectable
Might yet exceed in sweetness, O restore
The cherry-cobbler of the days of yore
Made only by Al Keefer's mother!—Why,
The very thought of it ignites the eye
Of memory with rapture—cloys the lip
Of longing, till it seems to ooze and drip
With veriest juice and stain and overwaste
Of that most sweet delirium of taste

That ever visited the childish tongue,
Or proved, as now, the sweetest thing unsung.

Ah, Almon Keefer! what a boy you were,
With your back-tilted hat and careless hair,
And open, honest, fresh, fair face and eyes
With their all-varying looks of pleased surprise
And joyous interest in flower and tree,
And poising humming-bird, and maundering bee.

The fields and woods he knew; the tireless tramp
With gun and dog; and the night-fisher's camp—
No other boy, save Bee Lineback, had won
Such brilliant mastery of rod and gun.
Even in his earliest childhood had he shown
These traits that marked him as his father's own.
Dogs all paid Almon honor and bow-wowed
Allegiance, let him come in any crowd
Of rabbit-hunting town-boys, even though
His own dog "Sleuth" rebuked their acting so
With jealous snarls and growlings.

                              But the best
Of Almon's virtues—leading all the rest—
Was his great love of books, and skill as well
In reading them aloud, and by the spell

28

Thereof enthralling his mute listeners, as
They grouped about him in the orchard-grass,
Hinging their bare shins in the mottled shine
And shade, as they lay prone, or stretched supine
Beneath their favorite tree, with dreamy eyes
And Argo-fancies voyaging the skies.
"Tales of the Ocean" was the name of one
Old dog's-eared book that was surpassed by none
Of all the glorious list.—Its back was gone,
But its vitality went bravely on
In such delicious tales of land and sea
As may not ever perish utterly.
Of still more dubious caste, "Jack Sheppard"
      drew
Full admiration; and "Dick Turpin," too.
And, painful as the fact is to convey,
In certain lurid tales of their own day,
These boys found thieving heroes and outlaws
They hailed with equal fervor of applause:
"The League of the Miami"—why, the name
Alone was fascinating—is the same,
In memory, this venerable hour
Of moral wisdom shorn of all its power,
As it unblushingly reverts to when
The old barn was "the Cave," and hears again

29

The signal blown, outside the buggy-shed—
The drowsy guard within uplifts his head,
And "'*Who goes there?*'" is called, in bated
    breath—
The challenge answered in a hush of death,—
"Sh!—'*Barney Gray!*'" And then "'*What do
    you seek?*'"
"'*Stables of The League!*'" the voice comes spent
    and weak,
For, ha! the *Law* is on the "Chieftain's" trail—
Tracked to his very lair!—Well, what avail?
The "secret entrance" opens—closes.—So
The "Robber-Captain" thus outwits his foe;
And, safe once more within his "cavern-halls,"
He shakes his clinched fist at the warped plank-
    walls
And mutters his defiance through the cracks
At the balked Enemy's retreating backs
As the loud horde flees pell-mell down the lane,
And—*Almon Keefer* is himself again!

Excepting few, they were not books indeed
Of deep import that Almon chose to read;—
Less fact than fiction.—Much he favored those—
If not in poetry, in hectic prose—

That made our native Indian a wild,
Feathered and fine-preened hero that a child
Could recommend as just about the thing
To make a god of, or at least a king.

Aside from Almon's own books—two or three—
His store of lore The Township Library
Supplied him weekly: All the books with " or "s—
Subtitled—lured him—after "Indian Wars,"
And "Life of Daniel Boone,"—not to include
Some few books spiced with humor,—"Robin
    Hood"
And rare "Don Quixote."—And one time he took
"Dadd's Cattle Doctor." . . . How he hugged the
    book
And hurried homeward, with internal glee
And humorous spasms of expectancy!—
All this confession—as he promptly made
It, the day later, writhing in the shade
Of the old apple-tree with Johnty and
Bud, Noey Bixler, and The Hired Hand —
Was quite as funny as the book was not. . . .
O Wonderland of wayward Childhood! what
An easy, breezy realm of summer calm
And dreamy gleam and gloom and bloom and balm

31

Thou art!—The Lotus-Land the poet sung,
It is the Child-World while the heart beats
young. . . .

While the heart beats young!—O the splendor of the
Spring,
With all her dewy jewels on, is not so fair a thing!
The fairest, rarest morning of the blossom-time of
May
Is not so sweet a season as the season of to-day
While Youth's diviner climate folds and holds us, close
caressed,
As we feel our mothers with us by the touch of face
and breast;—
Our bare feet in the meadows, and our fancies up
among
The airy clouds of morning—while the heart beats
young.

While the heart beats young and our pulses leap and
dance,
With every day a holiday and life a glad romance,—
We hear the birds with wonder, and with wonder watch
their flight—
Standing still the more enchanted, both of hearing and
of sight,

32

When they have vanished wholly,—for, in fancy, wing-
to-wing
We fly to Heaven with them; and, returning, still we
sing
The praises of this *lower* Heaven with tireless voice and
tongue,
Even as the Master sanctions—while the heart beats
young.

While the heart beats young!—While the heart beats
young!
O green and gold old Earth of ours, with azure over-
hung
And looped with rainbows!—grant us yet this grassy
lap of thine—
We would be still thy children, through the shower
and the shine!
So pray we, lisping, whispering, in childish love and
trust,
With our beseeching hands and faces lifted from the
dust
By fervor of the poem, all unwritten and unsung,
Thou givest us in answer, while the heart beats young.

ANOTHER hero of those youthful years
Returns, as Noey Bixler's name appears.

And Noey—if in any special way—
Was notably good-natured.—Work or play
He entered into with selfsame delight—
A wholesome interest that made him quite
As many friends among the old as young,—
So everywhere were Noey's praises sung.

And he was awkward, fat and overgrown,
With a round full-moon face, that fairly shone
As though to meet the simile's demand.
And, cumbrous though he seemed, both eye and
        hand
Were dowered with the discernment and deft
        skill
Of the true artisan: He shaped at will,
In his old father's shop, on rainy days,
Little toy-wagons, and curved-runner sleighs;
The trimmest bows and arrows—fashioned, too,
Of "seasoned timber," such as Noey knew
How to select, prepare, and then complete,
And call his little friends in from the street.
"The very *best* bow," Noey used to say,
"Hain't made o' ash ner hick'ry thataway!—
But you git *mulberry*—the *bearin'*-tree,
Now mind ye! and you fetch the piece to me,

34

And lemme git it *seasoned;* then, i gum!
I'll make a bow 'at you kin brag on some!
Er—ef you can't git *mulberry,*—you bring
Me a' old *locus'* hitch-post, and, i jing!
I'll make a bow o' *that* 'at *common* bows
Won't dast to pick on ner turn up their nose!"

And Noey knew the woods, and all the trees
And thickets, plants and myriad mysteries
Of swamp and bottom-land.   And he knew where
The ground-hog hid, and why located there.—
He knew all animals that burrowed, swam,
Or lived in tree-tops: And, by race and dam,
He knew the choicest, safest deeps wherein
Fish-traps might flourish nor provoke the sin
Of theft in some chance peeking, prying sneak,
Or town-boy, prowling up and down the creek.
All four-pawed creatures tamable—he knew
Their outer and their inner natures too;
While they, in turn, were drawn to him as by
Some subtle recognition of a tie
Of love, as true as truth from end to end,
Between themselves and this strange human friend.
The same with birds—he knew them every one,
And he could "name them, too, without a gun."

No wonder *Johnty* loved him, even to
The verge of worship.—Noey led him through
The art of trapping redbirds—yes, and taught
Him how to keep them when he had them caught—
What food they needed, and just where to swing
The cage, if he expected them to *sing*.

And *Bua* loved Noey, for the little pair
Of stilts he made him; or the stout old hair
Trunk Noey put on wheels, and laid a track
Of scantling-railroad for it in the back
Part of the barn-lot; or the crossbow, made
Just like a gun, which deadly weapon laid
Against his shoulder as he aimed, and—"*Sping!*"
He'd hear the rusty old nail zoon and sing—
And *zip!* your Mr. Bluejay's wing would drop
A farewell-feather from the old tree-top!

And *Maymie* loved him, for the very small
But perfect carriage for her favorite doll—
A *lady's* carriage—not a *baby*-cab,—
But oil-cloth top, and two seats, lined with drab
And trimmed with white lace-paper from a case
Of shaving-soap his uncle bought some place
At auction once.

36

And *Alex* loved him yet
The best, when Noey brought him, for a pet,
A little flying-squirrel, with great eyes—
Big as a child's: And, childlike otherwise,
It was at first a timid, tremulous, coy,
Retiring little thing that dodged the boy
And tried to keep in Noey's pocket;—till,
In time responsive to his patient will,
It became wholly docile, and content
With its new master, as he came and went,—
The squirrel clinging flatly to his breast,
Or sometimes scampering its craziest
Around his body spirally, and then
Down to his very heels and up again.

And *Little Lizzie* loved him, as a bee
Loves a great ripe red apple—utterly.
For Noey's ruddy morning-face she drew
The window-blind, and tapped the window, too;
Afar she hailed his coming, as she heard
His tuneless whistling—sweet as any bird
It seemed to her, the one lame bar or so
Of old "Wait for the Wagon"—hoarse and low
The sound was,—so that, all about the place,
Folks joked and said that Noey "whistled bass"—

The light remark originally made
By Cousin Rufus, who knew notes, and played
The flute with nimble skill, and taste as well,
And, critical as he was musical,
Regarded Noey's constant whistling thus
"Phenomenally unmelodious."
Likewise when Uncle Mart, who shared the love
Of jest with Cousin Rufus hand-in-glove,
Said "Noey couldn't whistle '*Bonny Doon*'
Even! and, *he'd* bet, couldn't carry a tune
If it had handles to it!"

                              —But forgive
The deviations here so fugitive,
And turn again to Little Lizzie, whose
High estimate of Noey we shall choose
Above all others.—And to her he was
Particularly lovable because
He laid the woodland's harvest at her feet.—
He brought her wild strawberries, honey-sweet
And dewy-cool, in mats of greenest moss
And leaves, all woven over and across
With tender, biting "tongue-grass," and "sheep-
       sour,"
And twin-leaved beech-mast, pranked with bud and
       flower

Of every gypsy-blossom of the wild,
Dark, tangled forest, dear to any child.—
All these in season. Nor could barren, drear,
White and stark-featured Winter interfere
With Noey's rare resources: Still the same
He blithely whistled through the snow and came
Beneath the window with a Fairy sled;
And Little Lizzie, bundled heels-and-head,
He took on such excursions of delight
As even "Old Santy" with his reindeer might
Have envied her! And, later, when the snow
Was softening toward Springtime and the glow
Of steady sunshine smote upon it,—then
Came the magician Noey yet again—
While all the children were away a day
Or two at Grandma's!—and behold when they
Got home once more;—there, towering taller than
The doorway—stood a mighty, old Snow-Man!

A thing of peerless art—a masterpiece
Doubtless unmatched by even classic Greece
In heyday of Praxiteles.—Alone
It loomed in lordly grandeur all its own.
And steadfast, too, for weeks and weeks it stood,
The admiration of the neighborhood

As well as of the children Noey sought
Only to honor in the work he wrought.
The traveller paid it tribute, as he passed
Along the highway—paused and, turning, cast
A lingering, last look—as though to take
A vivid print of it, for memory's sake,
To lighten all the empty, aching miles
Beyond with brighter fancies, hopes and smiles.
The cynic put aside his biting wit
And tacitly declared in praise of it;
And even the apprentice-poet of the town
Rose to impassioned heights, and then sat down
And penned a panegyric scroll of rhyme
That made the Snow-Man famous for all time.

And though, as now, the ever warmer sun
Of summer had so melted and undone
The perishable figure that—alas!—
Not even in dwindled white against the grass
Was left its latest and minutest ghost,
The children yet—*materially*, almost—
Beheld it—circled round it hand-in-hand—
(Or rather round the place it used to stand)—
With "Ring-a-round-a-rosy! Bottle full
O' posy!" and, with shriek and laugh, would pull

40

From seeming contact with it—just as when
It was the *real-est* of old Snow-Men!

EVEN in such a scene of senseless play
The children were surprised one summer day
By a strange man who called across the fence,
Inquiring for their father's residence;
And, being answered that this was the place,
Opened the gate, and, with a radiant face,
Came in and sat down with them in the shade
And waited—till the absent father made
His noon appearance, with a warmth and zest
That told he had no ordinary guest
In this man whose low-spoken name he knew
At once, demurring as the stranger drew
A stuffy note-book out, and turned and set
A big fat finger on a page, and let
The writing thereon testify instead
Of further speech.   And as the father read
All silently, the curious children took
Exacting inventory both of book
And man:—He wore a long-napped white fur hat
Pulled firmly on his head, and under that
Rather long silvery hair, or iron-gray—
For he was not an old man,—anyway,

Not beyond sixty. And he wore a pair
Of square-framed spectacles—or rather there
Were two more than a pair,—the extra two
Flared at the corners, at the eyes' side-view,
In as redundant vision as the eyes
Of grasshoppers or bees or dragon-flies.
Later the children heard the father say
He was " A Noted Traveller," and would stay
Some days with them.—In which time host and guest
Discussed, alone, in deepest interest,
Some vague, mysterious matter that defied
The wistful children, loitering outside
The spare-room door. There Bud acquired a quite
New list of big words—such as " Disunite,"
And " Shibboleth," and " Aristocracy,"
And " Juggernaut," and " Squatter Sovereignty,"
And " Antislavery," " Emancipate,"
" Irrepressible Conflict," and " The Great
Battle of Armageddon "—obviously
A pamphlet brought from Washington, D. C.,
And spread among such friends as might occur
Of like views with " The Noted Traveller."

A PROSPECTIVE VISIT

WHILE *any* day was notable and dear
That gave the children Noey, history here
Records his advent emphasized indeed
With sharp italics, as he came to feed
The stock one special morning, fair and bright,
When Johnty and Bud met him, with delight
Unusual even as their extra dress—
Garbed as for holiday, with much excess
Of proud self-consciousness and vain conceit
In their new finery.—Far up the street
They called to Noey, as he came, that they,
As promised, both were going back that day
To *his* house with him!

                    And by time that each
Had one of Noey's hands—ceasing their speech
And coyly anxious, in their new attire,
To wake the comment of their mute desire,—

43

Noey seemed rendered voiceless.   Quite a while
They watched him furtively.—He seemed to smile
As though he would conceal it; and they saw
Him look away, and his lips purse and draw
In curious, twitching spasms, as though he might
Be whispering,—while in his eye the white
Predominated strangely.—Then the spell
Gave way, and his pent speech burst audible:
"They wuz two stylish little boys,
    and they wuz mighty bold ones,
Had two new pairs o' britches made
    out o' their Daddy's old ones!"
And at the inspirational outbreak,
Both joker and his victims seemed to take
An equal share of laughter,—and all through
Their morning visit kept recurring to
The funny words and jingle of the rhyme
That just kept getting funnier all the time.

AT NOEY'S HOUSE

At Noey's house—when they arrived with him—
How snug seemed everything, and neat and trim:
The little picket-fence, and little gate—
Its little pulley, and its little weight,—
All glib as clockwork, as it clicked behind
Them, on the little red-brick pathway, lined
With little paint-keg vases and tea-pots
Of wee moss-blossoms and forget-me-nots:
And in the windows, either side the door,
Were ranged as many little boxes more
Of like old-fashioned larkspurs, pinks and moss
And fern and phlox; while up and down across
Them rioted the morning-glory vines
On taut-set cotton strings, whose snowy lines
Whipped in and out and under the bright green
Like basting-threads; and, here and there between

A showy, shiny hollyhock would flare
Its pink among the white and purple there.—
And still behind the vines, the children saw
A strange, bleached, wistful face that seemed to
    draw
A vague, indefinite sympathy.   A face
It was of some newcomer to the place.—
In explanation, Noey, briefly, said
That it was "Jason," as he turned and led
The little fellows round the house to show
Them his menagerie of pets.   And so
For quite a time the face of the strange guest
Was partially forgotten, as they pressed
About the squirrel-cage and rousted both
The lazy inmates out, though wholly loath
To whirl the wheel for them.—And then with
    awe
They walked round Noey's big pet owl, and saw
Him film his great, clear, liquid eyes and stare
And turn and turn and turn his head round there
The same way they kept circling—as though he
Could turn it one way thus eternally.

Behind the kitchen, then, with special pride
Noey stirred up a terrapin inside

The rain-barrel where he lived, with three or four
Little mud-turtles of a size not more
In neat circumference than the tiny toy
Dumb-watches worn by every little boy.

Then, back of the old shop, beneath the tree
Of "rusty-coats," as Noey called them, he
Next took the boys, to show his favorite new
Pet coon—pulled rather coyly into view
Up through a square hole in the bottom of
An old inverted tub he bent above,
Yanking a little chain, with "Hey! you, sir!
Here's *comp'ny* come to see you, Bolivur!"
Explanatory, he went on to say,
"I named him *Bolivur* jes thisaway,—
He looks so *round* and *ovalish* and *fat*,
'Peared-like no other name 'ud fit but that."

Here Noey's father called and sent him on
Some errand. "Wait," he said—"I won't be gone
A half a' hour.—Take Bud, and go on in
Where Jason is, tel I git back ag'in."

WHOEVER *Jason* was, they found him there
Still at the front-room window.—By his chair

Leaned a new pair of crutches; and from one
Knee down, a leg was bandaged.—"Jason done
That-air with one o' these-'ere tools *we* call
A '*shin-hoe*'—but a *foot-adze* mostly all
Hardware-store-keepers calls 'em."—(*Noey* made
This explanation later.)

                Jason paid
But little notice to the boys as they
Came in the room:—An idle volume lay
Upon his lap—the only book in sight—
And Johnty read the title,—"Light, More Light,
There's Danger in the Dark,"—though *first* and
    best—
In fact, the *whole* of Jason's interest
Seemed centred on a little *dog*—one pet
Of Noey's all uncelebrated yet—
Though *Jason*, certainly, avowed his worth,
And niched him over all the pets on earth—
As the observant Johnty would relate
The *Jason*-episode, and imitate
The all-enthusiastic speech and air
Of Noey's kinsman and his tribute there:—

"THAT little dog 'ud scratch at that door
And go on a-whinin' two hours before
48

He'd ever let up! *There!*—Jane: Let him in.—
(Hah, there, you little rat!) Look at him grin!
Come down off o' that!—
            W'y, look at him! (*Drat
You! you-rascal-you!*)—bring me that hat!
Look *out!*—He'll snap *you!*—*He* wouldn't let
You take it away from him, now you kin bet!
That little rascal's jist natchurly mean.—
I tell you, I *never* (*Git out!!*), never seen
A *spunkier* little rip! (*Scratch to git in*,
And *now* yer a-scratchin' to git *out* ag'in!
Jane: Let him out.) Now, watch him from
      here
Out through the winder!—You notice one ear
Kindo' *in*side-*out*, like he holds it?—Well,
He's got a *tick* in it—*I* kin tell!
            Yes, and he's cunnin'—
            Jist watch him a-runnin',
Sidelin'—see!—like he ain't '*plum'd true*'
And legs don't 'track' as they'd ort to do!—
Ploughin' his nose through the weeds—i jing!
Ain't he jist cuter'n anything!

"W'y, that little dog's got *grown*-people's sense!—
See how he gits out under the fence?—

And watch him a-whettin' his hind legs 'fore
His dead square run of a mile'd er more—
'Cause *Noey's* a-comin', and Trip allus knows
When *Noey's* a-comin'—and off he goes!—
Putts out to meet him and—*There they come now!*
Well-sir! it's raially singalar how
   That dog kin *tell*,—
   But he knows as well
When Noey's a-comin' home !—Reckon his *smell*
'Ud carry two mile'd?—You needn't to *smile*—
He runs to meet *him*, ever'-once-'n-a-while,
Two mile'd and over—when he's slipped away
And left him at home here, as he's done to-
  day—
'Thout ever knowin' where Noey wuz goin'—
But that little dog allus hits the right way!
Hear him a-whinin' and scratchin' ag'in?—
(*Little tormentin' fice!*) Jane: Let him in.

  " —You say he ain't *there?*—
   Well now, I declare!—
Lem*me* limp out and look! . . . I wunder where—
Heuh, Trip!—*Heuh*, Trip!—*Heuh*, Trip! . . . *There*—
There he is!—Little sneak!—What-a'-you-'bout?—
There he is—quiled up as meek as a mouse,

50

His tail turnt up like a tea-kittle spout,
A-sunnin' hisse'f at the side o' the house!
Next time you scratch, sir, you'll haf to git in,
My fine little feller, the best way you kin!
—Noey *he* learns him sich capers!—And they—
Both of 'em's ornrier every day!—
Both tantalizin' and meaner'n sin—
Allus a—(*Listen there!*)—Jane: Let him in.

" —O! yer so *innocent!* hangin' yer head!—
(Drat ye! you'd *better* git under the bed!)
. . . Listen at that!—
He's tackled the cat!—
Hah, there! you little rip! come out o' that!—
Git yer blame' little eyes scratched out
'Fore you know what yer talkin' about!—
Here! come away from there!—(Let him alone—
He'll snap *you*, I tell ye, as quick as a bone!)
Hi, Trip!—*Hey*, here!—What-a'-you-'bout! —
Oo! ouch! 'Ll, I'll be blamed!—*Blast ye!* GIT OUT!
. . . O, it ain't nothin'—jist *scratched* me, you
see.—
Hadn't no idy he'd try to bite *me!*
Plague take him!—Bet he'll not try *that* ag'in!—
Hear him yelp.—(*Pore feller!*) Jane: Let him in."

51

THE LOEHRS AND THE HAMMONDS

"HEY, Bud! *O* Bud!" rang out a gleeful call,—
" *The Loehrs is come to your house!* " And a small
But very much elated little chap,
In snowy linen suit and tasselled cap,
Leaped from the back fence just across the street
From Bixlers', and came galloping to meet
His equally delighted little pair
Of playmates, hurrying out to join him there—
" *The Loehrs is come!—The Loehrs is come!* " his glee
Augmented to a pitch of ecstasy
Communicated wildly, till the cry
" *The Loehrs is come!* " in chorus quavered high
And thrilling as some pæan of challenge or
Soul-stirring chant of armied conqueror.
And who this *avant-courier* of "the Loehrs"?—
This happiest of all boys out o' doors—

Who but Will Pierson, with his heart's excess
Of summer warmth and light and breeziness!
"From our front winder I 'uz first to see
'Em all a-drivin' into town!" bragged he—
"An' seen 'em turnin' up the alley where
Your folks lives at.   An' John an' Jake wuz there
Both in the wagon;—yes, an' Willy, too;
An' Mary—yes, an' Edith—with bran-new
An' purtiest-trimmed hats 'at ever wuz!—
An' Susan, an' Janey.—An' the *Hammonds-uz*
In their fine buggy 'at they're ridin' roun'
So much, all over an' aroun' the town
An' *ever*'wheres,—them *city* people who's
A-visutin' at Loehrs-uz!"

                            Glorious news!—
Even more glorious when verified
In the boys' welcoming eyes of love and pride,
As one by one they greeted their old friends
And neighbors.—Nor until their earth-life ends
Will that bright memory become less bright
Or dimmed indeed.

                    . . . Again, at candle-light,
The faces all are gathered.   And how glad
The Mother's features, knowing that she had

Her dear, sweet Mary Loehr back again.—
She always was so proud of her; and then
The dear girl, in return, was happy, too,
And with a heart as loving, kind and true
As that maturer one which seemed to blend
As one the love of mother and of friend.
From time to time, as hand in hand they sat,
The fair girl whispered something low, whereat
A tender, wistful look would gather in
The mother-eyes; and then there would begin
A sudden cheerier talk, directed to
The stranger guests—the man and woman who,
It was explained, were coming now to make
Their temporary home in town for sake
Of the wife's somewhat failing health. Yes,
  they
Were city people, seeking rest this way,
The man said, answering a query made
By some well-meaning neighbor—with a shade
Of apprehension in the answer. . . . No,—
They had no *children*. As he answered so,
The man's arm went about his wife, and she
Leaned toward him, with her eyes lit prayerfully:
Then she arose—he following—and bent
Above the little sleeping innocent

Within the cradle at the mother's side—
He patting her, all silent, as she cried.—
Though, haply, in the silence that ensued,
His musings made melodious interlude.

In the warm, health-giving weather
    My poor pale wife and I
Drive up and down the little town
    And the pleasant roads thereby:
Out in the wholesome country
    We wind, from the main highway,
In through the wood's green solitudes—
    Fair as the Lord's own Day.

We have lived so long together,
    And joyed and mourned as one,
That each with each, with a look for speech,
    Or a touch, may talk as none
But Love's elect may comprehend—
    Why, the touch of her hand on mine
Speaks volume-wise, and the smile of her eyes,
    To me, is a song divine.

There are many places that lure us:—
    "The Old Wood Bridge" just west
Of town we know—and the creek below,
    And the banks the boys love best:

And "Beech Grove," too, on the hilltop;
　　And "The Haunted House" beyond,
With its roof half off, and its old pump-trough
　　Adrift in the roadside pond.

We find our way to "The marshes"—
　　At least where they used to be;
And "The Old Camp Grounds"; and "The Indian
　　　Mounds,"
　　And the trunk of "The Council Tree":
We have crunched and splashed through "Flint-bed
　　　Ford";
　　And at "Old Big Bee-gum Spring"
We have stayed the cup, half lifted up,
　　Hearing the redbird sing.

And then, there is "Wesley Chapel,"
　　With its little graveyard, lone
At the cross-roads there, though the sun sets fair
　　On wild rose, mound and stone. . . .
A wee bed under the willows—
　　My wife's hand on my own—
And our horse stops, too. . . . And we hear the coo
　　Of a dove in undertone.

The dusk, the dew, and the silence!
　　"Old Charley" turns his head

Homeward then by the pike again,
  Though never a word is said—
One more stop, and a lingering one—
  After the fields and farms,—
At the old Toll-Gate, with the woman await
  With a little girl in her arms.

The silence sank—Floretty came to call
The children in the kitchen, where they all
Went helter-skeltering with shout and din
Enough to drown most sanguine silence in,—
For well indeed they knew that summons meant
Taffy and pop-corn—so with cheers they went.

THE HIRED MAN AND FLORETTY

THE Hired Man's supper, which he sat before,
In near reach of the wood-box, the stove-door
And one leaf of the kitchen-table, was
Somewhat belated, and in lifted pause
His dexterous knife was balancing a bit
Of fried mush near the port awaiting it.

At the glad children's advent—gladder still
To find *him* there—" Jest tickled fit to kill
To see ye all!" he said, with unctuous cheer.—
" I'm tryin'-like to he'p Floretty here
To git things cleared away and give ye room
Accordin' to yer stren'th.   But I p'sume
It's a pore boarder, as the poet says,
That quarrels with his victuals, so I guess
I'll take another wedge o' that-air cake,
Florett', that you're a-*learnin'* how to bake."
He winked and feigned to swallow painfully.—

58

"Jest 'fore ye all come in, Floretty she
Was boastin' 'bout her *biscuits*—and they *air*
As good—sometimes—as you'll find anywhere.—
But, women gits to braggin' on their *bread*,
I'm s'picious 'bout their *pie*—as Danty said."
This raillery Floretty strangely seemed
To take as compliment, and fairly beamed
With pleasure at it all.

      —"Speakin' o' *bread*—
When she come here to live," The Hired Man said,—
"Never be'n out o' *Freeport* 'fore she come
Up here,—of course she needed *'sperience* some.—
So, one day, when yer Ma was goin' to set
The risin' fer some bread, she sent Florett'
To borry *leaven*, 'crost at Ryans'.—So,
She went and asked fer *twelve*.—She didn't *know*,
But thought, *whatever* 'twuz, that she could keep
One fer *herse'f*, she said. O she wuz deep!"

Some little evidence of favor hailed
The Hired Man's humor; but it wholly failed
To touch the serious Susan Loehr, whose air
And thought rebuked them all to listening there
To her brief history of the *city* man
And his pale wife—"A sweeter woman than
59

She ever saw!"—So Susan testified,—
And so attested all the Loehrs beside.—
So entertaining was the history, that
The Hired Man, in the corner where he sat
In quiet sequestration, shelling corn,
Ceased wholly, listening, with a face forlorn
As Sorrow's own, while Susan, John and Jake
Told of these strangers who had come to make
Some weeks' stay in the town, in hopes to gain
Once more the health the wife had sought in
    vain:
Their doctor, in the city, used to know
The Loehrs—Dan and Rachel—years ago,—
And so had sent a letter and request
For them to take a kindly interest
In favoring the couple all they could—
To find some home-place for them, if they would,
Among their friends in town.   He ended by
A dozen further lines, explaining why
His patient must have change of scene and air—
New faces, and the simple friendships there
With *them*, which might, in time, make her forget
A grief that kept her ever brooding yet
And wholly melancholy and depressed,—
Nor yet could she find sleep by night nor rest

By day, for thinking—thinking—thinking still
Upon a grief beyond the doctor's skill,—
The death of her one little girl.

"Pore thing!"
Floretty sighed, and with the turkey-wing
Brushed off the stove-hearth softly, and peered in
The kettle of molasses, with her thin
Voice wandering into song unconsciously—
In purest, if most witless, sympathy.—

"'Then sleep no more:
Around thy heart
Some ten-der dream may i-dlee play,
But mid-night song,
With mad-jick art,
Will chase that dree muh-way!'"

"That-air besetment of Floretty's," said
The Hired Man,—"*singin'*—she *inhairited*,—
Her *father* wuz addicted—same as her—
To singin'—yes, and played the dulcimer!
But—gittin' back,—I s'pose yer talkin' 'bout
Them *Hammondses*.   Well, Hammond he gits
     out
Pattents on things—inventions-like, I'm told—
And's got more money'n a house could hold!

And yit he can't git up no pattent-right
To do away with *dyin'*.—And he might
Be worth a *million*, but he couldn't find
Nobody sellin' *health* of any kind! . . .
But they's no thing onhandier fer *me*
To use than other people's misery.—
Floretty, hand me that-air skillet there
And lemme git 'er het up, so's them-air
Childern kin have their pop-corn."

                              It was good
To hear him now, and so the children stood
Closer about him, waiting.

                            "Things to *eat*,"
The Hired Man went on, "'smighty hard to
    beat!
Now, when *I* wuz a boy, we wuz so pore,
My parunts couldn't 'ford pop-corn no more
To pamper *me* with;—so, I hat to go
Without pop-corn—sometimes a *year* er so!—
And *suffer'n' saints!* how hungry I would git
Fer jest one other chance—like this—at it!
Many and many a time I've *dreamp'*, at night,
About pop-corn,—all bu'sted open white,
And hot, you know—and jest enough o' salt
And butter on it fer to find no fault—

Oomh!—Well! as I was goin' on to say,—
After a-*dreamin'* of it thataway,
Then havin' to wake up and find it's all
A *dream*, and hain't got no pop-corn at-tall,
Ner hain't *had* none—I'd think, ' *Well, where's
    the use!* '
And jest lay back and sob the plaster'n'
    loose!
And I have *prayed*, what*ever* happened, it
'Ud eether be pop-corn er death! . . . And yit
I've noticed—more'n likely so have you—
That things don't happen when you *want*
    'em to."

And thus he ran on artlessly, with speech
And work in equal exercise, till each
Tureen and bowl brimmed white. And then he
    greased
The saucers ready for the wax, and seized
The fragrant-steaming kettle, at a sign
Made by Floretty; and, each child in line,
He led out to the pump—where, in the dim
New coolness of the night, quite near to him
He felt Floretty's presence, fresh and sweet
As . . . dewy night-air after kitchen-heat.

There, still, with loud delight of laugh and jest,
They plied their subtle alchemy with zest—
Till, sudden, high above their tumult, welled
Out of the sitting-room a song which held
Them stilled in some strange rapture, listening
To the sweet blur of voices chorussing:—

. . . . . .

"'When twilight approaches the season
    That ever is sacred to song,
Does some one repeat my name over,
    And sigh that I tarry so long?
And is there a chord in the music
    That's missed when my voice is away?—
And a chord in each heart that awakens
    Regret at my wearisome stay-ay—
    Regret at my wearisome stay.'"

All to himself, The Hired Man thought—"Of course
They'll sing *Floretty* homesick!"

. . . O strange source

Of ecstasy! O mystery of Song!—
To hear the dear old utterance flow along:—

"' Do they set me a chair near the table
    When evening's home-pleasures are nigh?—
When the candles are lit in the parlor,
    And the stars in the calm azure sky.'" . . .

64

Just then the moonlight sliced the porch slantwise,
And flashed in misty spangles in the eyes
Floretty clinched, while through the dark—
    "I jing!"
A voice asked, "Where's that song '*you'd* learn
    to sing
Ef I sent you the *ballat?*'—which I done
Last I was home at Freeport.—S'pose you run
And git it—and we'll all go in to where
They'll know the notes and sing it fer ye there."
And up the darkness of the old stairway
Floretty fled, without a word to say—
Save to herself some whisper muffled by
Her apron, as she wiped her lashes dry.

Returning, with a letter, which she laid
Upon the kitchen-table while she made
A hasty crock of "float,"—poured thence into
A deep glass dish of iridescent hue
And glint and sparkle, with an overflow
Of froth to crown it, foaming white as snow.—
And then—pound-cake, and jelly-cake as rare,
For its delicious complement,—with air
Of Hebe mortalized, she led her van
Of votaries, rounded by The Hired Man.

THE EVENING COMPANY

WITHIN the sitting-room, the company
Had been increased in number.   Two or three
Young couples had been added: Emma King,
Ella and Mary Mathers—all could sing
Like veritable angels—Lydia Martin, too,
And Nelly Millikan.—What songs they knew!—

> "'*Ever of thee—wherever I may be,*
> *Fondly I'm drea-m-ing ever of thee!'*"

And with their gracious voices blend the grace
Of Warsaw Barnett's tenor; and the bass
Unfathomed of Wick Chapman—Fancy still
Can *feel*, as well as *hear* it, thrill on thrill,
Vibrating plainly down the backs of chairs
And through the wall and up the old hall-stairs.—
Indeed, young Chapman's voice especially
Attracted *Mr. Hammond.*—For, said he,

Waiving the most Elysian sweetness of
The *ladies'* voices—altitudes above
The *man's* for sweetness;—*but*—as *contrast,* would
Not Mr. Chapman be so very good
As, just now, to oblige *all* with—in fact,
Some sort of *jolly* song,—to counteract
In part, at least, the sad, pathetic trend
Of music *generally.* Which wish our friend
"The Noted Traveller" made second to
With heartiness—and so each, in review,
Joined in—until the radiant *basso* cleared
His wholly unobstructed throat and peered
Intently at the ceiling—voice and eye
As opposite indeed as earth and sky.—
Thus he uplifted his vast bass and let
It roam at large the memories booming yet:

"'Old Simon the Cellarer keeps a rare store
　　Of Malmsey and Malvoi-sie,
　Of Cyprus, and who can say how many more?—
　　But a chary old soul is he-e-ee—
　　　A chary old so-u-l is he!
　Of hock and Canary he never doth fail;
　And all the year round, there is brewing of ale;—
　Yet he never aileth, he quaintly doth say,
　While he keeps to his sober six flagons a day.'"

. . . And then the chorus—the men's voices
Warred in it—like a German Carnival.—
Even *Mrs*. Hammond smiled, as in her youth,
Hearing her husband.—And in veriest truth
"The Noted Traveller's" ever-present hat
Seemed just relaxed a little, after that,
As at conclusion of the Bacchic song
He stirred his "float" vehemently and long.

Then Cousin Rufus with his flute, and art
Blown blithely through it from both soul and heart—
Inspired to heights of mastery by the glad,
Enthusiastic audience he had
In the young ladies of a town that knew
No other flutist,—nay, nor *wanted* to,
Since they had heard *his* "Polly Hopkins
        Waltz,"
Or "Rickett's Hornpipe," with its faultless faults,
As rendered solely, he explained, "by ear,"
Having but heard it once, Commencement Year,
At "Old Ann Arbor."
                    Little Maymie now
Seemed "friends" with *Mr. Hammond*—anyhow,
Was lifted to his lap—where settled, she,
Enthroned thus, in her dainty majesty,

Gained *universal* audience—although
Addressing him alone:—"I'm come to show
You my new Red-blue pencil; and *she* says"—
(Pointing to *Mrs.* Hammond)—"that she guess'
You'll make a *picture* fer me."

     "And what *kind*
Of picture?" Mr. Hammond asked, inclined
To serve the child as bidden, folding square
The piece of paper she had brought him there.—
"I don't know," Maymie said—"only ist make
A *little dirl*, like me!"

     He paused to take
A sharp view of the child, and then he drew—
Awhile with red, and then awhile with blue—
The outline of a little girl that stood
In converse with a wolf in a great wood;
And she had on a hood and cloak of red—
As Maymie watched—"*Red Riding-Hood!*" she said.
"And who's '*Red Riding-Hood*'?"

     "W'y, don't *you* know?"
Asked little Maymie—

     But the man looked so
All uninformed, that little Maymie could
But tell him *all about* Red Riding-Hood.

69

W'Y, one time wuz a little-weenty dirl,
An' she wuz named Red Riding-Hood, 'cause her—
Her *Ma* she maked a little red cloak fer her
'At turnt up over her head.—An' it 'uz all
Ist one piece o' red cardinul 'at's like
The drate-long stockin's the storekeepers has.—
O! it 'uz purtiest cloak in all the world
An' *all* this town er anywheres they is!
An' so, one day, her Ma she put it on
Red Riding-Hood, she did—one day, she did—
An' it 'uz *Sund'y*—'cause the little cloak
It 'uz too nice to wear ist *ever'* day
An' *all* the time!—An' so her Ma, she put
It on Red Riding-Hood—an' telled her not
To dit no dirt on it ner dit it mussed
Ner nothin'!   An'—an'—nen her Ma she dot
Her little basket out, 'at Old Kriss bringed

70

Her wunst—one time, he did.   An' nen she fill'
It full o' whole lots an' 'bundance o' dood things t'
    eat
(Allus my Dran'ma *she* says ''bundance,' too.)
An' so her Ma fill' little Red Riding-Hood's
Nice basket all ist full o' dood things t' eat,
An' tell her take 'em to her old Dran'ma—
An' not to *spill* 'em, neever—'cause ef she
'Ud stump her toe an' spill 'em, her Dran'ma
She'll haf to *punish* her!

                            An' nen—An' so
Little Red Riding-Hood she p'omised she
'Ud be all careful nen, an' cross' her heart
'At she won't run an' spill 'em all fer six—
Five—ten—two-hunderd-bushel-dollars-gold!
An' nen she kiss her Ma doo'-bye an' went
A-skippin' off—away fur off frough the
Big woods, where her Dran'ma she live at—
    No!—
She didn't do *a-skippin'*, like I said:—
She ist went *walkin'*—careful-like an' slow—
Ist like a little lady—walkin' 'long
As all polite an' nice—an' slow—an' straight—
An' turn her toes—ist like she's marchin' in
The Sund'y-School k-session!

71

An'—an'—so

She 'uz a-doin' along—an' doin' along—
On frough the drate-big woods—'cause her Dran'ma
She live 'way, 'way fur off frough the big woods
From *her* Ma's house. So when Red Riding-Hood
Dit to do there, she allus have most fun—
When she do frough the drate-big woods, you
    know.—
'Cause she ain't feard a bit o' anything!
An' so she sees the little hoppty-birds
'At's in the trees, an' flyin' all around,
An' singin' dlad as ef their parunts said
They'll take 'em to the magic-lantern show!
An' she 'ud pull the purty flowers an' things
A-growin' round the stumps.—An' she 'ud ketch
The purty butterflies, an' drasshoppers,
An' stick pins frough 'em—No!—I ist *said* that!—
'Cause she's too dood an' kind an' 'bedient
To *hurt* things thataway.—She'd *ketch* 'em, though,
An' ist *play* wiv 'em ist a little while,
An' nen she'd let 'em fly away, she would,
An' ist skip on ad'in to her Dran'ma's.

An' so, while she 'uz doin' 'long an' 'long,
First thing you know they 'uz a drate-big old

72

Mean wicked Wolf jumped out 'at wanted t' eat
Her up, but *dassent* to—'cause wite clos't there
They wuz a Man a-choppin' wood, an' you
Could *hear* him.—So the old Wolf he 'uz *feard*
Only to ist be *kind* to her.—So he
Ist 'tended-like he wuz dood friends to her
An' says, "Dood morning, little Red Riding-Hood!"—
All ist as kind!

An' nen Riding-Hood
She say "Dood morning," too—all kind an' nice—
Ist like her Ma she learn'—No!—mustn't say
"Learn," 'cause "*learn*" it's unproper.—So she say
It like her *Ma* she "*teached*" her.—An'—so she
Ist says "Dood morning" to the Wolf—'cause she
Don't know ut-tall 'at he's a *wicked* Wolf
An' want to eat her up!

Nen old Wolf smile
An' say, so kind: "Where air you doin' at?"
Nen little Red Riding-Hood she say: "I'm doin'
To my Dran'ma's, 'cause my Ma say I might."
Nen, when she tell him that, the old Wolf he
Ist turn an' light out frough the big thick woods,
Where she can't see him any more.   An' so
She think he's went to *his* house—but he hain't,—
He's went to her Dran'ma's, to be there first—

73

An' *ketch* her, ef she don't watch mighty sharp
What she's about!
                An' nen when the old Wolf
Dit to her Dran'ma's house, he's purty smart,—
An' so he 'tend-like *he's* Red Riding-Hood,
An' knock at th' door. An' Riding-Hood's Dran'ma
She's sick in bed an' can't come to the door
An' open it. So th' old Wolf knock *two* times.
An' nen Red Riding-Hood's Dran'ma she says,
"Who's there?" she says. An' old Wolf 'tends-like
    he's
Little Red Riding-Hood, you know, an' make'
His voice soun' ist like hers, an' says: "It's me,
Dran'ma—an' I'm Red Riding-Hood an' I'm
Ist come to *see* you."
              Nen her old Dran'ma
She think it *is* little Red Riding-Hood,
An' so she say: "Well, come in nen an' make
You'se'f at home," she says, "'cause I'm down sick
In bed, an' got the 'ralgia, so's I can't
Dit up an' let ye in."
             An' so th' old Wolf
Ist march' in nen an' shet the door ad'in,
An' *drowl*, he did, an' *splunge* up on the bed
An' et up old Miz Riding-Hood 'fore she

74

Could put her specs on an' see who it wuz.—
An' so she never knowed *who* et her up!

An' nen the wicked Wolf he ist put on
Her nightcap, an' all covered up in bed—
Like he wuz *her*, you know.

　　　　　　　Nen, purty soon
Here come along little Red Riding-Hood,
An' *she* knock' at the door. An' old Wolf 'tend-
Like *he's* her Dran'ma; an' he say, "Who's there?"
Ist like her Dran'ma say, you know. An' so
Little Red Riding-Hood she say: "It's *me*,
Dran'ma—an' I'm Red Riding-Hood an' I'm
Ist come to *see* you."

　　　　　　　An' nen old Wolf nen
He cough an' say: "Well, come in nen an' make
You'se'f at home," he says, "'cause I'm down sick
In bed, an' got the 'ralgia, so's I can't
Dit up an' let ye in."

　　　　　　　An' so she think
It's her Dran'ma a-talkin'.—So she ist
Open' the door an' come in, an' set down
Her basket, an' taked off her things, an' bringed
A chair an' clumbed up on the bed, wite by
The old big Wolf she thinks is her Dran'ma—

Only she thinks the old Wolf's dot whole lots
More bigger ears, an' lots more whiskers, too,
Than her Dran'ma; an' so Red Riding-Hood
She's kindo' skeered a little.   So she says,
"Oh, Dran'ma, what *big eyes* you dot!"   An' nen
The old Wolf says: "They're ist big thataway
'Cause I'm so dlad to see you!"

                      Nen she says,
"Oh, Dran'ma, what a drate-big nose you dot!"
Nen th' old Wolf says: "It's ist big thataway
Ist 'cause I smell the dood things 'at you bringed
Me in the basket!"

                  An' nen Riding-Hood
She say, "Oh-me-oh-*my!* Dran'ma! what big
White long sharp teeth you dot!"

                      Nen old Wolf says:
"Yes—an' they're thataway"—an' drowled—
"They're thataway," he says, "to *eat* you wiv!"
An' nen he ist *jump* at her.—

                      But she *scream*—
An' *scream*, she did.—So's 'at the Man
'At wuz a-choppin' wood, you know,—*he* hear,
An' come a-runnin' in there wiv his axe;
An', 'fore the old Wolf know' what he's about,
He split his old brains out an' killed him s' quick

It make' his head swim!—An' Red Riding-Hood
She wuzn't hurt at all!

                 An' the big Man
He tooked her all safe home, he did, an' tell
Her Ma she's all right an' ain't hurt at all
An' old Wolf's dead an' killed—an' ever'thing!—
So her Ma wuz so tickled an' so proud,
She gived *him* all the good things t' eat they wuz
'At's in the basket, an' she tell him 'at
She's much oblige', an' say to " call ad'in."
An' story's honest *truth*—an' all *so*, too!

LIMITATIONS OF GENIUS

The audience entire seemed pleased—indeed,
Extremely pleased.   And little Maymie, freed
From her task of instructing, ran to show
Her wondrous colored picture to and fro
Among the company.
> "And how comes it," said
Some one to Mr. Hammond, "that, instead
Of the inventor's life, you did not choose
The *artist's?*—since the world can better lose
A cutting-box or reaper than it can
A noble picture painted by a man
Endowed with gifts this drawing would suggest"—
Holding the picture up to show the rest.
"*There now!*" chimed in the wife, her pale face lit
Like winter snow with sunrise over it,—
"That's what *I'm* always asking him.—But *he*—
Well, as he's answering *you*, he answers *me*,—

With that same silent, suffocating smile
He's wearing now!"
              For quite a little while
No further speech from any one, although
All looked at Mr. Hammond and that slow,
Immutable, mild smile of his.   And then
The encouraged querist asked him yet again
Why was it, and etcetera—with all
The rest, expectant, waiting round the wall,—
Until the gentle Mr. Hammond said
He'd answer with a "*parable,*" instead—
About "a dreamer" that he used to know—
"An artist"—"master"—*all*—in *embryo.*

MR. HAMMOND'S PARABLE

THE DREAMER

I

HE was a Dreamer of the Days:
  Indolent as a lazy breeze
Of midsummer, in idlest ways
  Lolling about in the shade of trees.
The farmer turned—as he passed him by
  Under the hillside where he kneeled
Plucking a flower—with scornful eye
  And rode ahead in the harvest-field
Muttering—"Lawz! ef that-air shirk
  Of a boy wuz mine fer a week er so,
He'd quit *dreamin'* and git to work
  And *airn* his livin'—er—Well! *I* know!"
And even kindlier rumor said,
Tapping with finger a shaking head,—

"Got such a curious kind o' way—
Wouldn't surprise me much, I say!"

Lying limp, with upturned gaze
Idly dreaming away his days.
No companions? Yes, a book
Sometimes under his arm he took
To read aloud to a lonesome brook.
    And school-boys, truant, once had heard
A strange voice chanting, faint and dim—
Followed the echoes, and found it him,
    Perched in a tree-top like a bird,
Singing, clean from the highest limb;
And, fearful and awed, they all slipped by
To wonder in whispers if he could fly.

"Let him alone!" his father said
    When the old schoolmaster came to say,
    "He took no part in his books to-day—
Only the lesson the readers read.—
    His mind seems sadly going astray!"
"Let him alone!" came the mournful tone,
And the father's grief in his sad eyes shone—
Hiding his face in his trembling hand,
Moaning, "Would I could understand!

81

But as Heaven wills it I accept
Uncomplainingly!" So he wept.

Then went "The Dreamer" as he willed,
As uncontrolled as a light sail filled
Flutters about with an empty boat
Loosed from its moorings and afloat:
Drifted out from the busy quay
Of dull school-moorings listlessly;
Drifted off on the talking breeze,
All alone with his reveries;
Drifted on, as his fancies wrought—
Out on the mighty gulfs of thought.

II

The farmer came in the evening gray
    And took the bars of the pasture down;
Called to the cows in a coaxing way,
    "Bess" and "Lady" and "Spot" and "Brown,"
While each gazed with a wide-eyed stare,
As though surprised at his coming there—
Till another tone, in a higher key,
Brought their obeyance loathfully.

    Then, as he slowly turned and swung
    The topmost bar to its proper rest,
        Something fluttered along and clung

An instant, shivering at his breast—
    A wind-scared fragment of legal cap
Which darted again, as he struck his hand
    On his sounding chest with a sudden slap,
And hurried sailing across the land.
But as it clung he had caught the glance
Of a little pencilled countenance,
And a glamour of written words; and hence,
A minute later, over the fence,
"Here and there and gone astray
Over the hills and far away,"
He chased it into a thicket of trees
And took it away from the captious breeze.

A scrap of paper with a rhyme
Scrawled upon it of summer-time:
A pencil-sketch of a dairymaid,
Under a farm-house porch's shade,
Working merrily; and was blent
With her glad features such sweet content,
That a song she sang in the lines below
Seemed delightfully apropos:—

SONG

  "Why do I sing—Tra-la-la-la-la!
    Glad as a King?—Tra-la-la-la-la!

Well, since you ask,—
    I have such a pleasant task,
I cannot help but sing!

"Why do I smile—Tra-la-la-la-la!
    Working the while?—Tra-la-la-la-la!
        Work like this is play,—
            So I'm playing all the day—
    I cannot help but smile!

"So, if you please—Tra-la-la-la-la!
    Live at your ease!—Tra-la-la-la-la!
        You've only got to turn,
            And, you see, it's bound to churn—
    It cannot help but please!"

The farmer pondered and scratched his head,
    Reading over each mystic word.—
"Some o' the Dreamer's work!" he said—
    "Ah, here's more—and name and date
In his handwrite'!"—And the good man read,—
    "'Patent applied for, July third,
    Eighteen hundred and forty-eight'!"
The fragment fell from his nerveless grasp—
His awed lips thrilled with the joyous gasp:
    "I see the p'int to the whole concern,—
    He's studied out a patent churn!"

84

FLORETTY'S MUSICAL CONTRIBUTION

ALL seemed delighted, though the elders more,
Of course, than were the children.—Thus, before
Much interchange of mirthful compliment,
The story-teller said *his* stories "went"
(Like a bad candle) *best* when they went *out*,—
And that some sprightly music, dashed about,
Would *wholly* quench his "glimmer," and inspire
Far brighter lights.
                         And, answering this desire,
The flutist opened, in a rapturous strain
Of rippling notes—a perfect April-rain
Of melody that drenched the senses through;—
Then—gentler—gentler—as the dusk sheds dew,
It fell, by velvety, staccatoed halts,
Swooning away in old "Von Weber's Waltz."
Then the young ladies sang "Isle of the Sea"—
In ebb and flow and wave so billowy,—
Only with quavering breath and folded eyes
The listeners heard, buoyed on the fall and rise
Of its insistent and exceeding stress
Of sweetness and ecstatic tenderness. . . .

With lifted finger *yet*, Remembrance—List!—
"*Beautiful isle of the sea!*" wells in a mist
Of tremulous. . . .
        . . . After much whispering
Among the children, Alex came to bring
Some kind of *letter*—as it seemed to be—
To Cousin Rufus.   This he carelessly
Unfolded—reading to himself alone,—
But, since its contents became, later, known,
And no one "*plagued* so *awful* bad," the same
May here be given—of course without full name,
Facsimile, or written kink or curl
Or clue.   It read:—

        " Wild Roved an indian Girl
     Brite al Floretty "
             deer freind
               i now take
~~this~~ These means to send that *Song* to you & make
my Promus good to you in the Regards
Of doing What i Promust afterwards.
the *notes* & *Words* is both here *Printed* sos
you ~~kin~~ can git *uncle Mart* to read you ~~them~~ those
& cousin Rufus you can git to *Play*
the *notes* fur you on eny Plezunt day
His Legul Work aint ~~Presein~~ Pressing.
                Ever thine

As shore as the Vine
doth the Stump intwine
thou art my Lump of Sackkerrine
  Rinaldo Rinaldine
  the Pirut in Captivity.

     . . . There dropped
Another square scrap.—But the hand was stopped
That reached for it—Floretty suddenly
Had set a firm foot on her property—
Thinking it was the *letter*, not the *song*,—
But blushing to discover she was wrong,
When, with all gravity of face and air,
Her precious letter *handed* to her there
By Cousin Rufus left her even more
In apprehension than she was before.
But, testing his unwavering, kindly eye,
She seemed to put her last suspicion by,
And, in exchange, handed the song to him.—

A page torn from a song-book: Small and dim
Both notes and words were—but as plain as day
They seemed to him, as he began to play—
And plain to *all* the singers,—as he ran
An airy, warbling prelude, then began
Singing and swinging in so blithe a strain,
That every voice rang in the old refrain:

MOUNTAIN MAID'S INVITATION

ARRANGED BY J. E. GOULD.

1. Come! come! come! O'er the hills, free from care, In my home true plea-sure share; Blos-soms sweet, flow'rs most rare, Come where joys are found! Here the spar-kling dews of morn Tree and shrub with gems a - dorn, Jew-els bright, gay-ly worn, Beau - ty all a - round! Tra la la la,

88

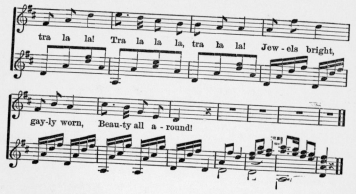

tra la la! Tra la la la, tra la la! Jew-els bright,

gay-ly worn, Beau-ty all a-round!

II

Come! come! come!
Not a sigh, not a tear,
E'er is found in sadness here;
Music soft, breathing near,
    Charms away each care!
Birds, in joyous hours, among
Hill and dell, with grateful song,
Dearest strains here prolong,
    Vocal all the air!
    Tra la la la, tra la la!
    Tra la la la, tra la la!
Dearest strains here prolong,
    Vocal all the air!

III

Come! come! come!
When the day's gently gone,
Evening shadows coming on,
Then, by love, kindly won,
    Truest bliss be thine!
Ne'er was found a bliss so pure,
Never joys so long endure;
Who would not love secure?
    Who would joys decline?
    Tra la la la, tra la la!
    Tra la la la, tra la la,
Who would not love secure?
    Who would joys decline?

89

From the beginning of the song, clean through,
Floretty's features were a study to
The flutist who "read *notes*" so readily,
Yet read so little of the mystery
Of that face of the girl's.—Indeed, *one* thing
Bewildered him quite into worrying,
And that was, noticing, throughout it all,
The Hired Man shrinking closer to the wall,
She ever backing toward him through the
    throng
Of barricading children—till the song
Was ended, and at last he saw her near
Enough to reach and take him by the ear
And pinch it just a pang's worth of her ire
And leave it burning like a coal of fire.
He noticed, too, in subtle pantomime
She seemed to dust him off, from time to time;
And when somebody, later, asked if she
Had never heard the song before—"What!
    me?"
She said—then blushed again and smiled,—
"I've knowed that song sence *Adam* wuz a child!—
It's jes a joke o' this-here man's.—He's learned
To *read* and *write* a little, and it's turned
His fool-head some—That's all!"

And then some one
Of the loud-wrangling boys said—"'*Course* they's none

No more, *these* days!—They's Fairies *ust* to be,
But they're all dead, a hunderd years!" said he.

"Well, there's where you're *mustakened!*"—in reply
They heard Bud's voice, pitched sharp and thin and high.—

"An' how you goin' to *prove* it?"

"Well, I *kin!*"
Said Bud, with emphasis,—"They's one lives in
Our garden—and I *see* 'im wunst, wiv my
Own eyes—*one* time I did."

"*Oh, what a lie!*"
—"'*Sh!*"

"Well, nen," said the skeptic—seeing there
The older folks attracted—"tell us *where*
You saw him, an' all '*bout* him!"

"Yes, my son.—
If you tell 'stories,' you may tell us one,"
The smiling father said, while Uncle Mart,
Behind him, winked at Bud, and pulled apart

His nose and chin with comical grimace—
Then sighed aloud, with sanctimonious face,—
    " ' *How good and comely it is to see*
    Children and parents in friendship agree! ' —
You fire away, Bud, on your Fairy tale—
Your *Uncle's* here to back you!"

       Somewhat pale,

And breathless as to speech, the little man
Gathered himself.   And thus his story ran.

BUD'S FAIRY TALE

SOME peoples thinks they ain't no Fairies *now*
No more yet!—But they *is*, I bet!   'Cause ef
They *wuzn't* Fairies, nen I' like to know
Who'd w'ite 'bout Fairies in the books, an' tell
What Fairies *does*, an' how their *picture* looks,
An' all an' ever'thing!   W'y, ef they don't
Be Fairies any more, nen little boys
'Ud ist *sleep* when they go to sleep an' won't
Have ist no dweams at all,—'cause Fairies—*good*
Fairies—they're a-purpose to make dweams!
But they *is* Fairies—an' I *know* they is!
'Cause one time wunst, when it's all Summer-time,
An' don't haf to be no fires in the stove
Er fireplace to keep warm wiv—ner don't haf
To wear old scwatchy flannen shirts at all,

An' ain't no fweeze—ner cold—ner snow!—An'—an'
Old skweeky twees got all the gween leaves on
An' ist keeps noddin', noddin' all the time,
Like they 'uz lazy an' a-twyin' to go
To sleep an' couldn't, 'cause the wind won't quit
A-blowin' in 'em, an' the birds won't stop
A-singin', so's they *kin*.—But twees *don't* sleep,
I guess!   But *little boys* sleeps—an' *dweams*, too.—
An' that's a sign they's Fairies.
                              So, one time,
When I be'n playin' "Store" wunst over in
The shed of their old stable, an' Ed Howard
He maked me quit a-bein' pardners, 'cause
I dwinked the 'tend-like sody-water up
An' et the shore-'nuff crackers,—w'y, nen I
Clumbed over in our garden where the gwapes
Wuz purt'-nigh ripe: An' I wuz ist a-layin'
There on th' old cwooked seat 'at Pa maked in
Our arber,—an' so I 'uz layin' there
A-whittlin' beets wiv my new dog-knife, an'
A-lookin' wite up thue the twimbly leaves—
An' wuzn't 'sleep at all!—An'-sir!—first thing
You know, a little *Fairy* hopped out there!—
A *leetle-teenty Fairy!*—*hope-may-die!*
An' he look' down at me, he did—an' he

Ain't bigger'n a *yellerbird!*—an' he
Say "Howdy-do!" he did—an' I could *hear*
Him—ist as *plain!*

        Nen *I* say "Howdy-do!"
An' he say "*I'm* all hunky, Nibsey; how
Is *your* folks comin' on?"

              An' nen I say
"My name ain't '*Nibsey*,' neever—my name's *Bud.*—
An' what's *your* name?" I says to him.

                  An' he
Ist laugh an' say, "'*Bud's*' awful *funny* name!"
An' he ist laid back on a big bunch o' gwapes
An' laugh' an' laugh', he did—like somebody
'Uz tick-el-un his feet!

           An' nen I say—
"What's *your* name," nen I say, "afore you bu'st
Yo'se'f a-laughin' 'bout *my* name?" I says.
An' nen he dwy up laughin'—kindo' mad—
An' say, "W'y, *my* name's *Squidjicum*," he says.
An' nen *I* laugh an' say—"*Gee!* what a name!"
An' when I make fun of his name, like that,
He ist git awful mad an' spunky, an'
'Fore you know, he gwabbed holt of a vine—
A big long vine 'at's danglin' up there, an'
He ist helt on wite tight to that, an' down

He swung quick past my face, he did, an' ist
Kicked at me hard's he could!
                                   But I'm too quick
Fer *Mr. Squidjicum!*   I ist weached out
An' ketched him, in my hand—an' helt him, too,
An' *squeezed* him, ist like little wobins when
They can't fly yet an' git flopped out their nest.
An' nen I turn him all wound over, an'
Look at him clos't, you know—wite clos't,—'cause ef
He *is* a Fairy, w'y, I want to see
The *wings* he's got.—But he's dwessed up so fine
'At I can't *see* no wings.—An' all the time
He's twyin' to kick me yet: An' so I take
F'esh holts an' *squeeze* ag'in—an' harder, too;
An' I says, " *Hold up, Mr. Squidjicum!*—
You're kickin' the w'ong man!" I says; an' nen
I ist *squeeze'* him, purt'-nigh my *best,* I did—
An' I heerd somepin' bu'st!—An' nen he cwied
An' says, "You better look out what you're doin'!—
You' bu'st my spider-web suspenners, an'
You' got my wose-leaf coat all cwinkled up
So's I can't go to old Miss Hoodjicum's
Tea-party, 's afternoon!"
                                   An' nen I says—
"Who's ' old Miss Hoodjicum '?" I says.

An' he
Says, "Ef you lemme loose I'll tell you."

So
I helt the little skeezics 'way fur out
In one hand—so's he can't jump down t' th' ground
Wivout a-gittin' all stove up: an' nen
I says, "You're loose now.—Go ahead an' tell
'Bout the 'tea-party' where you're goin' at
So awful fast!" I says.

An' nen he say,—
"No use to *tell* you 'bout it, 'cause you won't
Believe it, 'less you go there your own se'f
An' see it wiv your own two eyes!" he says.
An' *he* says: "Ef you lemme *shore-'nuff* loose,
An' p'omise 'at you'll keep wite still, an' won't
Tetch nothin' 'at you see—an' never tell
Nobody in the world—an' lemme loose—
W'y, nen I'll *take* you there!"

But I says, "Yes
An' ef I let you loose, you'll *run!*" I says.
An' he says, "No, I won't!—I hope-may-die!"
Nen I says, "Cwoss your heart you won't!"

An' he
Ist cwoss his heart; an' nen I reach an' set
The little feller up on a long vine—
97

An' he 'uz so tickled to git loose ag'in,
He gwab the vine wiv boff his little hands
An' ist take an' turn in, he did, an' skin
'Bout forty-'leben cats!

               Nen when he git
Thue whirlin' wound the vine, an' set on top
Of it ag'in, w'y, nen his "wose-leaf coat"
He bwag so much about, it's ist all tored
Up, an' ist hangin' strips an' rags—so he
Look like his Pa's a dwunkard. An' so nen
When he see what he's done—a-actin' up
So smart,—he's awful mad, I guess; an' ist
Pout out his lips an' twis' his little face
Ist ugly as he kin, an' set an' tear
His whole coat off—an' sleeves an' all.—An' nen
He wad it all togevver an' ist *th'ow*
It at me ist as hard as he kin dwive!

An' when I weach to ketch him, an' 'uz goin'
To give him 'nuvver squeezin', *he ist flewed
Clean up on top the arber!*—'Cause, you know,
They *wuz* wings on him—when he tored his *coat*
Clean off—they *wuz* wings *under there.* But they
Wuz purty wobbly-like an' wouldn't work
Hardly at all—'cause purty soon, when I

98

Th'owed clods at him, an' sticks, an' got him shooed
Down off o' there, he come a-floppin' down
An' lit k-bang! on our old chicken-coop,
An' ist laid there a-whimper'n' like a child!
An' I tiptoed up wite clos't, an' I says, "What's
The matter wiv ye, Squidjicum?"

                                An' he
Says: "Dog-gone! when my wings gits stwaight
        ag'in,
Where you all *cwumpled* 'em," he says, "I bet
I'll ist fly clean away an' won't take you
To old Miss Hoodjicum's at all!" he says.
An' nen I ist weach out wite quick, I did,
An' gwab the sassy little snipe ag'in—
Nen tooked my top-stwing an' tie down his wings
So's he *can't* fly, 'less'n I want him to!
An' nen I says: "Now, Mr. Squidjicum,
You better ist light out," I says, "to old
Miss Hoodjicum's, an' show *me* how to git
There, too," I says; "er ef you don't," I says,
"I'll climb up wiv you on our buggy-shed
An' push you off!" I says.

                                An' nen he say
All wite, he'll show me there; an' tell me nen
To set him down wite easy on his feet,

An' loosen up the stwing a little where
It cut him under th' arms.   An' nen he says,
"Come on!" he says; an' went a-limpin' 'long
The garden-paph—an' limpin' 'long an' 'long
Tel—purty soon he come on 'long to where's
A grea'-big cabbage-leaf.   An' he stoop down
An' say, "Come on inunder here wiv me!"
So *I* stoop down an' crawl inunder there,
Like he say.
        An' inunder there's a grea'-
Big clod, they is—a' awful grea'-big clod!
An' nen he says, "*woll this-here clod away!*"
An' so I woll' the clod away.   An' nen
It's all wet, where the dew'z inunder where
The old clod wuz.—An' nen the Fairy he
Git on the wet-place: Nen he say to me,
"Git on the wet-place, too!"   An' nen he say,
"Now hold yer breff an' shet yer eyes!" he says,
"Tel I say *Squinchy-winchy!*"   Nen he say—
Somepin' *in Dutch*, I guess.—An' nen I felt
Like we 'uz sinkin' down—an' sinkin' down!—
Tel purty soon the little Fairy weach
An' pinch my nose an' yell at me an' say,
"*Squinchy-winchy!   Look wherever you please!*"
Nen when I looked—Oh! they 'uz purtiest place

Down there you ever saw in all the World!—
They 'uz ist *flowers* an' *woses*—yes, an' *twees*
Wiv *blossoms* on an' *big wipe apples* boff!
An' butterflies, they wuz—an' hummin'-birds—
An' *yeller*birds an' *blue*birds—yes, an' *wed!*—
An' ever'wheres an' all awound 'uz vines
Wiv wipe p'serve-pears on 'em!—Yes, an' all
An' ever'thing 'at's ever gwowin' in
A garden—er canned up—all wipe at wunst!—
It wuz ist like a garden—only it
'Uz ist a *little bit* o' garden—'bout big wound
As ist our twun'el-bed is.—An' all wound
An' wound the little garden's a gold fence—
An' little gold gate, too—an' ash-hopper
'At's all gold, too—an' ist full o' gold ashes!
An' wite in th' middle o' the garden wuz
A little gold house, 'at's ist 'bout as big
As ist a bird-cage is: An' *in* the house
They 'uz whole-lots *more* Fairies there—'cause I
Picked up the little house, an' peeked in at
The winders, an' I see 'em all in there
Ist *buggin'* round!   An' Mr. Squidjicum
He twy to make me quit, but I gwab *him*
An' poke him down the chimbly, too, I did!—
An' y'ort to see *him* hop out 'mongst 'em there!—

Ist like he 'uz the boss an' ist got back!—
" *Hain't ye got on them-air dew-dumplin's yet?* "
He says.

   An' they says no.

      An' nen he says—
" *Better git at 'em nen!* " he says, " *wite quick—
'Cause old Miss Hoodjicum's a-comin'!* "

         Nen
They all set wound a little gold tub—an'
All 'menced a-peelin' dewdwops, ist like they
'Uz *peaches.*—An', it looked so funny, I
Ist laugh' out loud, an' *dwopped* the little house,—
An' 't bu'sted like a soap-bubble!—An' 't skeered
Me so, I—I—I—I,—it skeered me so,—
I—ist *waked* up.—No! I *ain't* be'n *asleep*
An' *dweam* it all, like *you* think,—but it's shore
Fer-certain *fact* an' cwoss my heart it is!

A DELICIOUS INTERRUPTION

ALL were quite gracious in their plaudits of
Bud's Fairy; but another stir above
That murmur was occasioned by a sweet
Young lady-caller, from a neighboring street,
Who rose reluctantly to say good night
To all the pleasant friends and the delight
Experienced,—as she had promised sure
To be back home by nine.   Then paused, demure,
And wondered was it *very* dark.—Oh, *no!*—
She had *come* by herself and she could go
Without an *escort*.   Ah, you sweet girls all!
What young gallant but comes at such a call,
Your most abject of slaves!   Why, there were three
Young men, and several men of family,
Contesting for the honor—which at last
Was given to Cousin Rufus; and he cast
A kingly look behind him, as the pair
Vanished with laughter in the darkness there.

As order was restored, with everything
Suggestive, in its way, of "romancing,"
Some one observed that *now* would be the chance
For *Noey* to relate a circumstance
That *he*—the very specious rumor went—
Had been eye-witness of, by accident.
Noey turned pippin-crimson; then turned pale
As death; then turned to flee, without avail.—
" *There!* head him off! *Now!* hold him in his chair!—
Tell us the Serenade-tale, now, Noey.—*There!* "

NOEY'S NIGHT-PIECE

"THEY ain't much 'tale' about it!" Noey said.—
"K'tawby grapes wuz gittin' good-'n'-red
I rickollect; and Tubb Kingry and me
'Ud kindo' browse round town, daytime, to see
What neighbers 'peared to have the most to spare
'At wuz git-at-able and no dog there
When we come round to git 'em, say 'bout ten
O'clock at night, when mostly old folks then
Wuz snorin' at each other like they yit
Helt some old grudge 'at never slep' a bit.
Well, at the *Pars'nige*—ef ye'll call to mind,—
They's 'bout the biggest grape-arber you'll find
'Most anywheres.—And mostly there, we knowed
They wuz *k'tawbies* thick as ever growed—
And more'n they'd *p'serve.*—Besides I've heerd
Ma say k'tawby-grape p'serves jes 'peared
A waste o' sugar, anyhow!—And so
My conscience stayed outside and lemme go

With Tubb, one night, the back-way, clean up
    through
That long black arber to the end next to
The house, where the k'tawbies, don't you know,
Wuz thickest.   And 't'uz lucky we went *slow*,—
Fer jes as we wuz cropin' to'rds the gray-
End, like, of the old arber—heerd Tubb say
In a skeered whisper, 'Hold up! They's some one
Jes slippin' in here!—and *looks like a gun*
He's carryin'!'   I *golly!* we both spread
Out flat ag'inst the ground!
                         'What's that?' Tubb said.—
And jes then—'*plink! plunk! plink!*' we heerd
    something
Under the back-porch winder.—Then, i jing!
Of course we rickollected 'bout the young
School-mam 'at wuz a-boardin' there, and sung,
And played on the melodium in the choir.—
And she 'uz 'bout as purty to admire
As any girl in town!—the fac's is, she
Jes *wuz*, them times, to a dead certainty,
The belle o' this-here bailywick!—But—Well,—
I'd best git back to what I'm tryin' to tell:—
It wuz some feller come to serenade
Miss Wetherell: And there he plunked and played

His old guitar, and sung, and kep' his eye
Set on her winder, blacker'n the sky!—
And black it *stayed*.—But mayby she wuz 'way
From home, er wore out—bein' *Saturday!*

"It *seemed* a good 'eal *longer*, but I *know*
He sung and plunked there half a' hour er so
Afore, it 'peared-like, he could ever git
His own free qualified consents to quit
And go off 'bout his business.   When he went
I bet you could 'a' bought him fer a cent!

"And now, behold ye all!—as Tubb and me
Wuz 'bout to raise up,—right in front we see
A feller slippin' out the arber, square
Smack under that-air little winder where
The *other* feller had been standin'.—And
The thing he wuz a-carryin' in his hand
Wuzn't no *gun* at all!—It wuz a *flute*,—
And *whoop-ee!* how it did git up and toot
And chirp and warble, tel a mockin'-bird
'Ud dast to never let hisse'f be heerd
Ferever, after sich miracalous, high
Jimcracks and grand skyrootics played there by

Yer Cousin Rufus!—Yes-sir; it wuz him!—
And what's more,—all a-suddent that-air dim
Dark winder o' Miss Wetherell's wuz lit
Up like a' oyshture-sign, and under it
We see him sorto' wet his lips and smile
Down 'long his row o' dancin' fingers, while
He kindo' stiffened up and kinked his breath
And everlastin'ly jes blowed the peth
Out o' that-air old one-keyed flute o' his.
And, bless their hearts, that's all the 'tale' they is!"

And even as Noey closed, all radiantly
The unconscious hero of the history,
Returning, met a perfect driving storm
Of welcome—a reception strangely warm
And *unaccountable*, to *him*, although
Most *gratifying*,—and he told them so.
"I only urge," he said, "my right to be
Enlightened." And a voice said: "*Certainly:*—
During your absence we agreed that you
Should tell us all a story, old or new,
Just in the immediate happy frame of mind
We knew you would return in."

                              So, resigned,
The ready flutist tossed his hat aside—
Glanced at the children, smiled, and thus complied.

108

COUSIN RUFUS' STORY

My little story, Cousin Rufus said,
Is not so much a story as a fact.
It is about a certain wilful boy—
An aggrieved, unappreciated boy,
Grown to dislike his own home very much,
By reason of his parents being not
At all up to his rigid standard and
Requirements and exactions as a son
And disciplinarian.

So, sullenly
He brooded over his disheartening
Environments and limitations, till,
At last, well knowing that the outside world
Would yield him favors never found at home,
He rose determinedly one July dawn—
Even before the call for breakfast—and,
Climbing the alley-fence, and bitterly
Shaking his clinched fist at the woodpile, he

Evanished down the turnpike.—Yes: he had,
Once and for all, put into execution
His long low-muttered threatenings—He had
Run off!—He had—had run away from home!

His parents, at discovery of his flight,
Bore up first-rate—especially his Pa,—
Quite possibly recalling his own youth,
And therefrom predicating, by high noon,
The absent one was very probably
Disporting his nude self in the delights
Of the old swimmin'-hole, some hundred yards
Below the slaughter-house, just east of town.
The stoic father, too, in his surmise
Was accurate—For, lo! the boy was there!

And there, too, he remained throughout the day—
Save at one starving interval in which
He clad his sunburnt shoulders long enough
To shy across a wheat-field, shadow-like,
And raid a neighboring orchard—bitterly,
And with spasmodic twitchings of the lip,
Bethinking him how all the other boys
Had *homes* to go to at the dinner-hour—
While *he*—alas!—*he had no home!*—At least
These very words seemed rising mockingly,

110

Until his every thought smacked raw and sour
And green and bitter as the apples he
In vain essayed to stay his hunger with.
Nor did he join the glad shouts when the boys
Returned rejuvenated for the long
Wet revel of the feverish afternoon.—
Yet, bravely, as his comrades splashed and swam
And spluttered, in their weltering merriment,
He tried to laugh, too,—but his voice was hoarse
And sounded to him like some other boy's.
And then he felt a sudden, poking sort
Of sickness at the heart, as though some cold
And scaly pain were blindly nosing it
Down in the dreggy darkness of his breast.
The tensioned pucker of his purple lips
Grew ever chillier and yet more tense—
The central hurt of it slow spreading till
It did possess the little face entire.
And then there grew to be a knuckled knot—
An aching kind of core within his throat—
An ache, all dry and swallowless, which seemed
To ache on just as bad when he'd pretend
He didn't notice it as when he did.
It was a kind of a conceited pain—
An overbearing, self-assertive and

Barbaric sort of pain that clean outhurt
A boy's capacity for suffering—
So, many times, the little martyr needs
Must turn himself all suddenly and dive
From sight of his hilarious playmates and
Surreptitiously weep under water.

Thus

He wrestled with his awful agony
Till almost dark; and then, at last—then, with
The very latest lingering group of his
Companions, he moved turgidly toward home—
Nay, rather *oozed* that way, so slow he went,—
With loathful, hesitating, loitering,
Reluctant, late-election-returns air,
Heightened somewhat by the conscience-made
resolve
Of chopping a double armful of wood
As he went in by rear way of the kitchen.
And this resolve he executed;—yet
The hired girl made no comment whatsoever,
But went on washing up the supper-things,
Crooning the unutterably sad song, " *Then think,*
Oh, think how lonely this heart must ever be! "
Still, with affected carelessness, the boy
Ranged through the pantry; but the cupboard-door

Was locked.   He sighed then like a wet forestick
And went out on the porch.—At least the pump,
He prophesied, would meet him kindly and
Shake hands with him and welcome his return!
And long he held the old tin dipper up—
And oh, how fresh and pure and sweet the draught!
Over the upturned brim, with grateful eyes
He saw the back-yard, in the gathering night,
Vague, dim and lonesome; but it all looked good:
The lightning-bugs, against the grape-vines, blinked
A sort of sallow gladness over his
Home-coming, with this softening of the heart.
He did not leave the dipper carelessly
In the milk-trough.—No: he hung it back upon
Its old nail thoughtfully—even tenderly.
All slowly then he turned and sauntered toward
The rain-barrel at the corner of the house,
And, pausing, peered into it at the few
Faint stars reflected there.   Then—moved by some
Strange impulse new to him—he washed his feet.
He then went in the house—straight on into
The very room where sat his parents by
The evening lamp.—The father all intent
Reading his paper, and the mother quite
As intent with her sewing.   Neither looked

Up at his entrance—even reproachfully,—
And neither spoke.
                    The wistful runaway
Drew a long, quavering breath, and then sat down
Upon the extreme edge of a chair.   And all
Was very still there for a long, long while.—
Yet everything, someway, seemed *restful*-like
And *homy* and old-fashioned, good and kind,
And sort of *kin* to him!—Only too *still!*
If somebody would *say* something—just *speak*—
Or even rise up suddenly and come
And lift him by the ear sheer off his chair—
Or box his jaws—Lord bless 'em!—*anything!*—
Was he not there to thankfully accept
Any reception from parental source
Save this incomprehensible *voicelessness?*
O but the silence held its very breath!
If but the ticking clock would only *strike*
And for an instant drown the whispering,
Lisping, sifting sound the katydids
Made outside in the grassy nowhere!
                                    Far

Down some back-street he heard the faint halloo
Of boys at their night-game of "Town-fox,"
But now with no desire at all to be

Participating in their sport.—No; no;—
Never again in this world would he want
To join them there!—he only wanted just
To stay in home of nights—Always—always—
Forever and a day!

        He moved; and coughed—
Coughed hoarsely, too, through his rolled tongue;
    and yet
No vaguest of parental notice or
Solicitude in answer—no response—
No word—no look.   O it was deathly still!—
So still it was that really he could not
Remember any prior silence that
At all approached it in profundity
And depth and density of utter hush.
He felt that he himself must break it: So,
Summoning every subtle artifice
Of seeming nonchalance and native ease
And naturalness of utterance to his aid,
And gazing raptly at the house-cat where
She lay curled in her wonted corner of
The hearth-rug, dozing, he spoke airily
And said: "I see you've got the same old cat!"

BEWILDERING EMOTIONS

THE merriment that followed was subdued—
As though the story-teller's attitude
Were dual, in a sense, appealing quite
As much to sorrow as to mere delight,
According, haply, to the listener's bent
Either of sad or merry temperament.—
"And of your two appeals I much prefer
The pathos," said "The Noted Traveller,"—
"For should I live to twice my present years,
I know I could not quite forget the tears
That child-eyes bleed, the little palms nailed wide,
And quivering soul and body crucified. . . .
But, bless them! there are no such children here
To-night, thank God!—Come here to me, my dear!"
He said to little Alex, in a tone
So winning that the sound of it alone

Had drawn a child more loathful to his knee:—
"And, now-sir, *I'll* agree if *you'll* agree,—
You tell us all a story, and then *I*
Will tell one."

    "*But I can't.*"

        "Well, can't you *try?*"
"Yes, Mister: he *kin* tell *one*. Alex, tell
The one, you know, 'at you made up so well,
About the *Bear*. He allus tells that one,"
Said Bud,—"He gits it mixed some 'bout the *gun*
An' *axe* the Little Boy had, an' *apples*, too."—
Then Uncle Mart said—"There, now! that'll do!—
Let *Alex* tell his story his own way!"
And Alex, prompted thus, without delay
Began.

117

THE BEAR STORY

THAT ALEX "IST MAKED UP HIS-OWN-SE'F"

W'Y, wunst they wuz a Little Boy went out
In the woods to shoot a Bear.   So, he went out
'Way in the grea'-big woods—he did.—An' he
Wuz goin' along—an' goin' along, you know,
An' purty soon he heerd somepin' go " *Wooh!* "—
Ist thataway—" *Woo-ooh!* "   An' he wuz *skeered*,
He wuz.   An' so he runned an' clumbed a tree—
A grea'-big tree, he did,—a sicka-*more* tree.
An' nen he heerd it ag'in: an' he looked round,
An' *'t'uz a Bear!—a grea'-big shore-'nuff Bear!*—
No: 't'uz *two* Bears, it wuz—two grea'-big Bears—
One of 'em wuz—ist *one's* a *grea'-big* Bear.—
But they ist *boff* went " *Wooh!* "—An' here *they* come
To climb the tree an' git the Little Boy
An' eat him up!

118

An' nen the Little Boy
He 'uz skeered worse'n ever! An' here come
The grea'-big Bear a-climbin' th' tree to git
The Little Boy an' eat him up—Oh, *no!*—
It 'uzn't the *Big* Bear 'at clumb the tree—
It 'uz the *Little* Bear.   So here *he* come
Climbin' the tree—an' climbin' the tree!   Nen when
He git wite *clos't* to the Little Boy, w'y, nen
The Little Boy he ist pulled up his gun
An' *shot* the Bear, he did, an' killed him dead!
An' nen the Bear he falled clean on down out
The tree—away clean to the ground, he did—
Spling-splung! he falled *plum* down, an' killed him,
   too!
An' lit wite side o' where the *Big* Bear's at.

An' nen the Big Bear's awful mad, you bet!—
'Cause—'cause the Little Boy he shot his gun
An' killed the *Little* Bear.—'Cause the *Big* Bear
He—he 'uz the Little Bear's Papa.—An' so here
He come to climb the big old tree an' git
The Little Boy an' eat him up!   An' when
The Little Boy he saw the *grea'-big Bear*
A-comin', he 'uz badder skeered, he wuz,
Than *any* time!   An' so he think he'll climb

Up *higher*—'way up higher in the tree
Than the old *Bear* kin climb, you know.—But he—
He *can't* climb higher 'an old *Bears* kin climb,—
'Cause Bears kin climb up higher in the trees
Than any little Boys in all the Wo-r-r-ld!

An' so here come the grea'-big Bear, he did,—
A-climbin' up—an' up the tree, to git
The Little Boy an' eat him up!   An' so
The Little Boy he clumbed on higher, an' higher,
An' higher up the tree—an' higher—an' higher—
An' higher'n iss-here *house* is!—An' here come
The old Bear—clos'ter to him all the time!—
An' nen—first thing you know,—when th' old Big
   Bear
Wuz wite clos't to him—nen the Little Boy
Ist jabbed his gun wite in the old Bear's mouf
An' shot an' killed him dead!—No; I *fergot*,—
He didn't shoot the grea'-big Bear at all—
'Cause *they 'uz no load in the gun*, you know—
'Cause when he shot the *Little* Bear, w'y, nen
No load 'uz any more nen *in* the gun!

But th' Little Boy clumbed *higher* up, he did—
He clumbed *lots* higher—an' on up *higher*—an' higher
An' *higher*—tel he ist *can't* climb no higher,

120

'Cause nen the limbs 'uz all so little, 'way
Up in the teeny-weeny tiptop of
The tree, they'd break down wiv him ef he don't
Be keerful!   So he stop an' think: An' nen
He look around—An' here come the old Bear!
An' so the Little Boy make up his mind
He's got to ist git out o' there *some*way!—
'Cause here come the old Bear!—so clos't, his bref's
Purt'-nigh so's he kin feel how hot it is
Ag'inst his bare feet—ist like old "Ring's" bref
When he's be'n out a-huntin' an' 's all tired.
So when th' old Bear's so clos't—the Little Boy
Ist gives a grea'-big jump fer *'nother* tree—
No!—no, he don't do that!—I tell you what
The Little Boy does:—W'y, nen—w'y, he—Oh, *yes!*—
The Little Boy *he finds a hole up there*
'At's in the tree—an' climbs in there an' *hides*—
An' *nen* th' old Bear can't find the Little Boy
At all!—But purty soon the old Bear finds
The Little Boy's *gun* 'at's up there—'cause the *gun*
It's too *tall* to tooked wiv him in the hole.
So, when the old Bear find' the *gun*, he knows
The Little Boy's ist *hid* round *somers* there,—
An' th' old Bear 'gins to snuff an' sniff around,
An' sniff an' snuff around—so's he kin find

Out where the Little Boy's hid at.—An' nen—nen—
Oh, *yes!*—W'y, purty soon the old Bear climbs
'Way out on a big limb—a grea'-long limb,—
An' nen the Little Boy climbs out the hole
An' takes his axe an' chops the limb off! . . . Nen
The old Bear falls *k-splunge!* clean to the ground,
An' bu'st an' kill hisse'f plum dead, he did!

An' nen the Little Boy he git his gun
An' 'menced a-climbin' down the tree ag'in—
No!—no, he *didn't* git his *gun*—'cause when
The *Bear* falled, nen the *gun* falled, too—An' broked
It all to pieces, too!—An' *nicest* gun!—
His Pa ist buyed it!—An' the Little Boy
Ist cried, he did; an' went on climbin' down
The tree—an' climbin' down—an' climbin' down!—
An'-sir! when he 'uz purt'-nigh down,—w'y, nen
The old Bear he jumped up ag'in!—an' he
Ain't dead at all—*ist* 'tendin' thataway,
So he kin git the Little Boy an' eat
Him up!   But the Little Boy he 'uz too smart
To climb clean *down* the tree.—An' the old Bear
He can't climb *up* the tree no more—'cause when
He fell, he broke one of his—He broke *all*
His legs!—an' nen he *couldn't* climb!   But he

Ist won't go 'way an' let the Little Boy
Come down out of the tree. An' the old Bear
Ist growls round there, he does—ist growls an' goes
" *Wooh!—woo-ooh!* " all the time! An' Little Boy
He haf to stay up in the tree—all night—
An' 'thout no *supper* neever!—Only they
Wuz *apples* on the tree!—An' Little Boy
Et apples—ist all night—an' cried—an' cried!
Nen when 't'uz morning the old Bear went " *Wooh!* "
Ag'in, an' try to climb up in the tree
An' git the Little Boy—But he *can't*
Climb t' save his *soul*, he can't!—An' *oh!* he's *mad!*—
He ist tear up the ground! an' go " *Woo-ooh!* "
An'—*Oh, yes!*—purty soon, when morning's come
All *light*—so's you kin *see*, you know,—w'y, nen
The old Bear finds the Little Boy's *gun*, you know,
'At's on the ground.—(An' it ain't broke at all—
I ist *said* that!) An' so the old Bear think
He'll take the gun an' *shoot* the Little Boy:—
But *Bears they* don't know much 'bout shootin' guns:
So when he go to shoot the Little Boy,
The old Bear got the *other* end the gun
Ag'in' his shoulder, 'stid o' *th' other* end—
So when he try to shoot the Little Boy,
It shot *the Bear*, it did—an' killed him dead!

An' nen the Little Boy clumb down the tree
An' chopped his old woolly head off.—Yes, an' killed
The *other* Bear ag'in, he did—an' killed
All *boff* the bears, he did—an' tuk 'em home
An' *cooked* 'em, too, an' *et* 'em!

—An' that's all.

THE PATHOS OF APPLAUSE

THE greeting of the company throughout
Was like a jubilee,—the children's shout
And fusillading hand-claps, with great guns
And detonations of the older ones,
Raged to such tumult of tempestuous joy,
It even more alarmed than pleased the boy;
Till, with a sudden twitching lip, he slid
Down to the floor and dodged across and hid
His face against his mother as she raised
Him to the shelter of her heart, and praised
His story in low whisperings, and smoothed
The "amber-colored hair," and kissed and soothed
And lulled him back to sweet tranquillity—
"An' 'at's a sign 'at you're the Ma fer me!"
He lisped, with gurgling ecstasy, and drew
Her closer, with shut eyes; and feeling, too,
If he could only *purr* now like a cat,
He would undoubtedly be doing that!

125

" And now"—the serious host said, lifting there
A hand entreating silence;—" now, aware
Of the good promise of our Traveller guest
To add some story with and for the rest,
I think I favor you, and him as well,
Asking a story I have heard him tell,
And know its truth, in each minute detail ":
Then leaning on his guest's chair, with a hale
Hand-pat by way of full indorsement, he
Said, " Yes—the Free-Slave story—certainly."

The old man, with his waddy note-book out,
And glittering spectacles, glanced round about
The expectant circle, and still firmer drew
His hat on, with a nervous cough or two:
And, save at times the big hard words, and tone
Of gathering passion—all the speaker's own,—
The tale that set each childish heart astir
Was thus told by " The Noted Traveller."

TOLD BY "THE NOTED TRAVELLER"

COMING, clean from the Maryland-end
Of this great National Road of ours,
Through your vast West; with the time to spend,
Stopping for days in the main towns, where
Every citizen seemed a friend,
And friends grew thick as the wayside flowers,—
I found no thing that I might narrate
More singularly strange or queer
Than a thing I found in your sister-State
Ohio,—at a river-town—down here
In my note-book: *Zanesville—situate*
On the stream Muskingum—broad and clear,
And navigable, through half the year,
North, to Coshocton; south, as far
As Marietta.—But these facts are
Not of the *story*, but the *scene*
Of the simple little tale I mean

To tell *directly*—from this, straight through
To the *end* that is best worth listening to:

Eastward of Zanesville, two or three
Miles from the town, as our stage drove in,
I on the driver's seat, and he
Pointing out this and that to me,—
On beyond us—among the rest—
A grovy slope, and a fluttering throng
Of little children, which he "guessed"
Was a picnic, as we caught their thin
High laughter, as we drove along,
Clearer and clearer. Then suddenly
He turned and asked, with a curious grin,
What were my views on *Slavery?* "*Why?*"
I asked, in return, with a wary eye.
"Because," he answered, pointing his whip
At a little, whitewashed house and shed
On the edge of the road by the grove ahead,—
"Because there are two slaves *there*," he said—
"Two Black slaves that I've passed each trip
For eighteen years.—Though they've been set free,
They have been slaves ever since!" said he.
And, as our horses slowly drew
Nearer the little house in view,

All briefly I heard the history
Of this little old Negro woman and
Her husband, house, and scrap of land;
How they were slaves and had been made free
By their dying master, years ago
In old Virginia; and then had come
North here into a *free* State—so,
Safe forever, to found a home—
For themselves alone?—for they left South
    there
Five strong sons, who had, alas!
All been sold ere it came to pass
This first old master with his last breath
Had freed the *parents*.—(He went to death
Agonized and in dire despair
That the poor slave *children* might not share
Their parents' freedom.   And wildly then
He moaned for pardon and died.   Amen!)

Thus, with their freedom, and little sum
Of money left them, these two had come
North, full twenty long years ago;
And, settling there, they had hopefully
Gone to work, in their simple way,
Hauling—gardening—raising sweet

Corn, and pop-corn.—Bird and bee
In the garden-blooms and the apple-tree
Singing with them throughout the slow
Summer's day, with its dust and heat—
The crops that thirst and the rains that fail;
Or in Autumn chill, when the clouds hung low,
And hand-made hominy might find sale
In the near town-market; or baking pies
And cakes, to range in alluring show
At the little window, where the eyes
Of the Movers' children, driving past,
Grew fixed, till the big white wagons drew
Into a halt that would sometimes last
Even the space of an hour or two—
As the dusty, thirsty travellers made
Their noonings there in the beeches' shade
By the old black Aunty's spring-house, where,
Along with its cooling draughts, were found
Jugs of her famous sweet spruce-beer,
Served with her gingerbread-horses there,
While Aunty's snow-white cap bobbed round
Till the children's rapture knew no bound,
As she sang and danced for them, quavering clear
And high the chant of her old slave-days—

"Oh, Lo'd, Jinny! my toes is so',
Dancin' on yo' sandy flo'!"

Even so had they wrought all ways
To earn the pennies, and hoard them, too,—
And with what ultimate end in view?—
They were saving up money enough to be
Able, in time, to buy their own
Five children back.

              Ah! the toil gone through!
And the long delays and the heartaches, too,
And self-denials that they had known!
But the pride and glory that was theirs
When they first hitched up their shackly cart
For the long, long journey South!—The start
In the first drear light of the chilly dawn,
With no friends gathered in grieving throng,—
With no farewells and favoring prayers;
But, as they creaked and jolted on,
Their chiming voices broke in song—

"'Hail, all hail! don't you see the stars a-fallin'?
    Hail, all hail! I'm on my way.
        Gideon * am
        A healin' ba'm—
    I belong to the blood-washed army.
        Gideon am
        A healin' ba'm—
           On my way!'"

* *Gilead*—evidently.—EDITOR.

131

And their *return!*—with their oldest boy
Along with them! Why, their happiness
Spread abroad till it grew a joy
Universal—It even reached
And thrilled the town till the *Church* was stirred
Into suspecting that wrong was wrong!—
And it stayed awake as the preacher preached
A *Real* "Love"-text that he had not long
To ransack for in the Holy Word.
And the son, restored, and welcomed so,
Found service readily in the town;
And, with the parents, sure and slow,
He went "saltin' de cole cash down."

So with the *next* boy—and each one
In turn, till *four* of the five at last
Had been bought back; and, in each case,
With steady work and good homes not
Far from the parents, *they* chipped in
To the family fund, with an equal grace.
Thus they managed and planned and wrought,
And the old folks throve—Till the night before
They were to start for the lone last son
In the rainy dawn—their money fast
Hid away in the house,—two mean,

132

Murderous robbers burst the door.
· · · Then, in the dark, was a scuffle—a fall—
An old man's gasping cry—and then
A woman's fife-like shriek.

· · · Three men
Splashing by on horseback heard
The summons: And in an instant all
Sprang to their duty, with scarce a word.
And they were *in time*—not only to save
The lives of the old folks, but to bag
Both the robbers, and buck-and-gag
And land them safe in the county jail—
Or, as Aunty said, with a blended awe
And subtlety,—"Safe in de calaboose whah
De dawgs cain't bite 'em!"

—So prevail
The faithful!—So had the Lord upheld
His servants of both deed and prayer,—
HIS the glory unparalleled—
Theirs the reward,—their every son
Free, at last, as the parents were!
And, as the driver ended there
In front of the little house, I said,
All fervently, "Well done! well done!"

At which he smiled, and turned his head,
And pulled on the leaders' lines, and—"See!"
He said,—"you can read old Aunty's sign?"
And, peering down through these specs of mine
On a little, square board-sign, I read:

"Stop, traveller, if you think it fit,
    And quench your thirst, for a-fi'-penny-bit.—
    The rocky spring is very clear,
    And soon converted into beer."

And, though I read aloud, I could
Scarce hear myself for laugh and shout
Of children—a glad multitude
Of little people, swarming out
Of the picnic-grounds I spoke about.—
And in their rapturous midst, I see
Again—through mists of memory—
An old black Negress laughing up
At the driver, with her broad lips rolled
Back from her teeth, chalk-white, and gums
Redder than reddest red-ripe plums.
He took from her hand the lifted cup
Of clear spring-water, pure and cold,
And passed it to me: And I raised my hat
And drank to her with a reverence that

My conscience knew was justly due
The old black face, and the old eyes, too—
The old black head, with its mossy mat
Of hair, set under its cap and frills
White as the snows on Alpine hills;
Drank to the old *black* smile, but yet
Bright as the sun on the violet,—
Drank to the gnarled and knuckled old
Black hands whose palms had ached and bled
And pitilessly been worn pale
And white almost as the palms that hold
Slavery's lash while the victim's wail
Fails as a crippled prayer might fail.—
Ay, with a reverence infinite,
I drank to the old black face and head—
The old black breast with its life of light—
The old black hide with its heart of gold.

HEAT-LIGHTNING

THERE was a curious quiet for a space
Directly following: and in the face
Of one rapt listener pulsed the flush and glow
Of the heat-lightning that pent passions throw
Long ere the crash of speech.—He broke the spell—
The host:—The Traveller's story, told so well,
He said, had wakened there within his breast
A yearning, as it were, to know *the rest*—
That all unwritten sequence that the Lord
Of Righteousness must write with flame and sword,
Some awful session of His patient thought.
Just then it was, his good old mother caught
His blazing eye—so that its fire became
But as an ember—though it burned the same.
It seemed to her, she said, that she had heard
It was the *Heavenly* Parent never erred,
And not the *earthly* one that had such grace:
"Therefore, my son," she said, with lifted face

And eyes, "let no one dare anticipate
The Lord's intent.   While *He* waits, *we* will
   wait."
And with a gust of reverence genuine
Then Uncle Mart was aptly ringing in—
   " ' *If the darkened heavens lower,*
      Wrap thy cloak around thy form;
   Though the tempest rise in power,
      God is mightier than the storm! ' "
Which utterance reached the restive children all
As something humorous.   And then a call
For *him* to tell a story, or to "say
A funny piece."   His face fell right away:
He knew no story worthy.   Then he must
Declaim for them: In that, he could not trust
His memory.   And then a happy thought
Struck some one, who reached in his vest and
   brought
Some scrappy clippings into light and said
There was a poem of Uncle Mart's he read
Last April in "The Sentinel."   He had
It there in print, and knew all would be glad
To hear it rendered by the author.

                              And,
All reasons for declining at command

Exhausted, the now helpless poet rose
And said: "I am discovered, I suppose.
Though I have taken all precautions not
To sign my name to any verses wrought
By my transcendent genius, yet, you see,
Fame wrests my secret from me bodily;
So I must needs confess I did this deed
Of poetry red-handed, nor can plead
One whit of unintention in my crime—
My guilt of rhythm and my glut of rhyme.—

"'Mæonides rehearsed a tale of arms,
    And Naso told of curious meta*murp*hoses;
Unnumbered pens have pictured woman's charms,
    While crazy *I*'ve made poetry *on purposes!*'

In other words, I stand convicted—need
I say—by my own doing, as I read."

UNCLE MART'S POEM

THE OLD SNOW-MAN

Ho! the old Snow-Man
  That Noey Bixler made!
He looked as fierce and sassy
  As a soldier on parade!—
'Cause Noey, when he made him,
  While we all wuz gone, you see,
He made him, jist a-purpose,
  Jist as fierce as he could be!—
    But when we all got *ust* to him,
      Nobody wuz afraid
    Of the old Snow-Man
      That Noey Bixler made!

'Cause Noey told us 'bout him
  And what he made him fer:—
He'd come to feed, that morning
  He found we wuzn't here;

And so the notion struck him,
    When we all come taggin' home
'T'ud *s'prise* us ef a' old Snow-Man
    'Ud meet us when we come!
So, when he'd fed the stock, and milked,
    And be'n back home, and chopped
His wood, and et his breakfast, he
    Jist grabbed his mitts and hopped
Right in on that-air old Snow-Man
    That he laid out he'd make
Er bu'st a trace *a-tryin'*—jist
    Fer old-acquaintance-sake!—
      But work like that wuz lots more fun,
      He said, than when he played!
      Ho! the old Snow-Man
      That Noey Bixler made!

He started with a big snowball,
    And rolled it all around;
And as he rolled, more snow 'ud stick
    And pull up off the ground.—
He rolled and rolled all round the yard—
    'Cause we could see the *track*,
All wher' the snow come off, you know,
    And left it wet and black.

He got the Snow-Man's *legs-part* rolled—
In front the kitchen-door,—
And then he hat to turn in then
And roll and roll some more!—
He rolled the yard all round ag'in,
And round the house, at that—
Clean round the house and back to wher'
The blame legs-half wuz at!
He said he missed his dinner, too—
Jist clean fergot and stayed
There workin'.   Ho! the old Snow-Man
That Noey Bixler made!

And Noey said he hat to *hump*
To git the *top-half* on
The *legs-half!*—When he *did*, he said,
His wind wuz purt'-nigh gone.—
He said, i jucks! he jist drapped down
There on the old porch-floor
And panted like a dog!—And then
He up! and rolled some more!—
The *last* batch—that wuz fer his head,—
And—time he'd got it right
And clumb and fixed it on, he said—
He hat to quit fer night!—

And *then*, he said, he'd kep' right on
    Ef they'd be'n any *moon*
To work by! So he crawled in bed—
    And *could* 'a' slep' tel *noon*,
        He wuz so plum wore out! he said,—
        But it wuz washin'-day,
        And hat to cut a cord o' wood
        'Fore he could git away!

But, last, he got to work ag'in,—
    With spade, and gouge, and hoe,
And trowel, too—(All tools 'ud do
    What *Noey* said, you know!)
He cut his eyebrows out like cliffs—
    And his cheek-bones and chin
Stuck *furder* out—and his old *nose*
    Stuck out as fur-ag'in!
He made his eyes o' walnuts,
    And his whiskers out o' this-
Here buggy-cushion stuffin'—*moss*,
    The teacher says it is.
And then he made a' old wood' gun,
    Set keerless-like, you know,
Acrost one shoulder—kindo' like
    Big Foot, er Adam Poe—

Er, mayby, Simon Girty,
   The dinged old Renegade!
Wooh! the old Snow-Man
   That Noey Bixler made!

And there he stood, all fierce and grim,
   A stern, heroic form:
What was the winter blast to him,
   And what the driving storm?—
What wonder that the children pressed
   Their faces at the pane
And scratched away the frost, in pride
   To look on him again?—
      What wonder that, with yearning bold,
         Their all of love and care
      Went warmest through the keenest cold
         To that Snow-Man out there!

But the old Snow-Man—
   What a dubious delight
He grew at last when Spring came on
   And days waxed warm and bright!—
Alone he stood—all kith and kin
   Of snow and ice were gone;—

UNCLE MART'S POEM

Alone, with constant tear-drops in
   His eyes and glittering on
His thin, pathetic beard of black—
   Grief in a hopeless cause!—
Hope—hope is for the man that *dies*—
   What for the man that *thaws!*
   O Hero of a hero's make!—
     Let *marble* melt and fade,
   But never *you*—you old Snow-Man
     That Noey Bixler made!

"LITTLE JACK JANITOR"

AND there, in that ripe Summer night, once more
A wintry coolness through the open door
And window seemed to touch each glowing face
Refreshingly; and, for a fleeting space,
The quickened fancy, through the fragrant air,
Saw snowflakes whirling where the rose-leaves were,
And sounds of veriest jingling bells again
Were heard in tinkling spoons and glasses then.

Thus Uncle Mart's old poem sounded young
And crisp and fresh and clear as when first sung,
Away back in the wakening of Spring,
When his rhyme and the robin, chorussing,
Rumored, in duo-fanfare, of the soon
Invading Johnny-jump-ups, with platoon
On platoon of sweet-williams, marshalled fine
To bloomèd blarings of the trumpet-vine.

The poet turned to whisperingly confer
A moment with "The Noted Traveller,"

145

Then left the room, tripped up the stairs, and then
An instant later reappeared again,
Bearing a little, lacquered box, or chest,
Which, as all marked with curious interest,
He gave to the old Traveller, who in
One hand upheld it, pulling back his thin
Black lustre coat-sleeves, saying he had sent
Up for his "Magic Box," and that he meant
To test it there—especially to show
The Children. "It is *empty now*, you know."—
He thumped it with his knuckles, so they heard
The hollow sound—"But lest it be inferred
It is not *really* empty, I will ask
Little Jack Janitor, whose pleasant task
It is to keep it ship-shape."

                                    Then he tried
And rapped the little drawer in the side,
And called out sharply, "Are you in there,
      Jack?"
And then a little, squeaky voice came back,—
"*Of course I'm in here—ain't you got the key
Turned on me!*"

                          Then the Traveller leisurely
Felt through his pockets, and at last took out
The smallest key they ever heard about!—

It wasn't any longer than a pin:
And this at last he managed to fit in
The little keyhole, turned it, and then cried,
"Is everything swept out clean there inside?"
"*Open the drawer and see! Don't talk so much;
Or else,*" the little voice squeaked, "*talk in Dutch—
You age me, asking questions!*"

       Then the man
Looked hurt, so that the little folks began
To feel so sorry for him, he put down
His face against the box and had to frown.—
"Come, sir!" he called,—"no impudence to *me!*—
You've swept out clean?"

      "*Open the drawer and see!*"
And so he drew the drawer out: Nothing there
But just the empty drawer, stark and bare.
He shoved it back again, with a sharp click.—

"*Ouch!*" yelled the little voice—"*unsnap it—quick!*—
You've got my nose pinched in the crack!"

       And then
The frightened man drew out the drawer again,
The little voice exclaiming, "*Jee-mun-nee!*—
Say what you want, but please don't murder me!"

"Well, then," the man said, as he closed the drawer
With care, "I want some cotton-batting for
My supper! Have you got it?"

                    And inside,

All muffled-like, the little voice replied,
"*Open the drawer and see!*"

                  And, sure enough,

He drew it out, filled with the cotton stuff.
He then asked for a candle to be brought
And held for him; and tuft by tuft he caught
And lit the cotton, and, while blazing, took
It in his mouth and ate it, with a look
Of purest satisfaction.

              "Now," said he,

"I've eaten the drawer empty, let me see
What this is in my mouth": And with both hands
He began drawing from his lips long strands
Of narrow silken ribbons, every hue
And tint;—and crisp they were and bright and
    new
As if just purchased at some Fancy-Store.
"And now, Bub, bring your cap," he said, "before
Something might happen!" And he stuffed the cap
Full of the ribbons. "*There*, my little chap,
Hold *tight* to them," he said, "and take them to

The ladies there, for they know what to do
With all such rainbow finery!"

        He smiled
Half sadly, as it seemed, to see the child
Open his cap first to his mother. . . . There
Was not a ribbon in it anywhere!
"*Jack Janitor!*" the man said sternly through
The Magic Box—"Jack Janitor, did *you*
Conceal those ribbons anywhere?"

        " *Well, yes,*"
The little voice piped—"*but you'd never guess
The place I hid 'em if you'd guess a year!*"

"Well, won't you *tell* me?"

        " *Not until you clear
Your mean old conscience,*" said the voice, "*and make
Me first do something for the Children's sake.*"

"Well, then, fill up the drawer," the Traveller said,
"With whitest white on earth and reddest red!—
Your terms accepted—Are you satisfied?"

"*Open the drawer and see!*" the voice replied.

"*Why, bless my soul!*"—the man said, as he drew
The contents of the drawer into view—

"LITTLE JACK JANITOR"

"It's level-full of *candy!*—Pass it round—
Jack Janitor sha'n't steal *that,* I'll be bound!"—
He raised and crunched a stick of it, and
     smacked
His lips.—"Yes, that *is* candy, for a fact!—
And it's all *yours!*"

              And how the children there

Lit into it!—O never anywhere
Was such a feast of sweetness!

                "And now, then,"

The man said, as the empty drawer again
Slid to its place, he bending over it,—
"Now, then, Jack Janitor, before we quit
Our entertainment for the evening, tell
Us where you hid the ribbons—can't you?"

                    "*Well,*"

The squeaky little voice drawled sleepily—
"*Under your old hat, maybe.—Look and see!*"

All carefully the man took off his hat:
But there was not a ribbon under that.—
He shook his heavy hair, and all in vain
The old white hat—then put it on again:
"Now, tell me, *honest,* Jack, where *did* you hide
The ribbons?"

"Under your hat," the voice replied.—
"Mind! I said 'under' and not 'in' it.—Won't
You ever take the hint on earth?—or don't
You want to show folks where the ribbons at?—
Law! but I'm sleepy!—Under—unner yer hat!"

Again the old man carefully took off
The empty hat, with an embarrassed cough,
Saying, all gravely, to the children: "You
Must promise not to *laugh*—you'll all *want* to—
When you see where Jack Janitor has dared
To hide those ribbons—when he might have spared
My feelings.—But no matter!—Know the worst—
Here are the ribbons, as I feared at first."—
And, quick as snap of thumb and finger, there
The old man's head had not a sign of hair,
And in his lap a wig of iron-gray
Lay, stuffed with all that glittering array
Of ribbons. . . . "Take 'em to the ladies—Yes.
Good night to everybody, and God bless
The Children."

        In a whisper no one missed
The Hired Man yawned: "He's a vantrilloquist."
.   .   .   .
So gloried all the night.   Each trundle-bed
And pallet was enchanted—each child-head

Was packed with happy dreams. And long before
The dawn's first far-off rooster crowed, the snore
Of Uncle Mart was stilled, as round him pressed
The bare arms of the wakeful little guest
That he had carried home with him. . . .

" I think,"

An awed voice said—" (No: I don't want a *dwink*.—
Lay still.)—I think ' The Noted Traveller' he
'S the inscrutibul-est man I ever see!"

THE DE VINNE PRESS